SEA TROUT

HOW TO CATCH THEM

SEA TROUT
HOW TO CATCH THEM

Charles Bingham

SWAN HILL PRESS

First published in the UK in 1998
by Swan Hill Press, an imprint of Airlife Publishing Ltd

British Library Cataloguing-in-Publication Data
   A catalogue record for this book
   is available from the British Library

ISBN 1 85310 894 4

Typeset by Servis Filmsetting Ltd., Manchester
Printed in Hong Kong

Swan Hill Press
an imprint of Airlife Publishing Ltd
101 Longden Road, Shrewsbury, SY3 9EB, England

Contents

Introduction

The deception of feeding brown trout by the gossamer presentation of an imitative floating fly relies upon observation by the angler. Find a rising trout, identify the insect upon which it is feeding and knot on an artificial of the same size. Then cast with delicacy, avoid drag and tighten as the fish goes down with the fly. The sequence depends upon eyesight.

The taking of salmon requires the angler to cast to many known lies, sometimes over many miles of river. If he is fishing the fly off a floating line, he may see the fish lift towards the surface, roll and turn away with the fly – only then does he raise the rod. Eyesight again.

Sea-trout fishing by fly in the dark is different. Touch is not all, but fingers on the fly line send messages from the seeking fly and transmit them to the fisherman. Sight is secondary to touch and hearing. I fish in the dark with my mouth open; the air, its softness, movement and temperature tell me of sea-trout moods. There is nothing quite like fishing for sea-trout in the dark – the angler comes close, in the use of his physical senses, to a wild predator.

To me, there are three game-fishing peaks: wild brown trout on dry fly; salmon by fly off a floating line; and sea-trout in the night. In these pusuits, my vestigial sixth sense flickers to life when I am standing alone, mid-river, after peal on a moonlit night.

Night sea-trout fishing is not for those making a start at fly fishing. If you cannot cast, tie your knots and handle the tackle by day, learn to do so by fishing for trout before you slide forward, rod in hand, into the dark river half an hour after the bats start to fly.

There are other ways – upstream dry fly by day, upstream wet fly by day in a spate or upstream wind, spinning, worming, dapping and wet fly on a loch – and all of these will be described. A method I have not included is the use of maggots. Not that maggots are ineffective – quite the reverse, in fact. But we should all do something to ensure continuing runs of migratory fish, and if we eschew maggots, many more sea-trout will pass us on their way upstream to spawn.

To give a taste of the fascination of night fishing, I will describe a day and a night on my Dartmoor river.

I start to think about sea-trout fishing in November at the stationers when I am buying the following year's calendar. This must show the phases of the moon; full and new moons bring spring tides, and with these high-water influxes into the estuary come sea-trout which press forward up the river. Three days later they reach my beat, five miles above the sea.

There are anglers who shun the moonlight, saying the darkest hours are best. But if you are night fishing for the first time, go for the moonlit nights; you will stumble less. Take care not to silhouette yourself against the moon; fish with its beams in your face. And be stealthy: imagine you are a burglar stealing a fish from the river.

Although there is little to be seen before mid-June, I start to climb riverside trees at the end of May. Then, looking down into the tail of the most productive pool on the river, nerve-tingling sights are revealed through polarized spectacles. I take care to creep towards the water, using the tree for cover, and climb koala fashion, pressed against the back of the trunk. By the third week they are always there, still grey shadows close to the river bed, comatose, not feeding, biding their time.

If there are three of four slim fish in a group, they are school peal, a West Country name for little sea-trout of about 12 oz on their first return to the river from the sea. Farther out, where the water is waist deep, in front of the wretched central boulder on which they snag my line, are the heart-stoppers, the 3- or 4-pounders. There are not many of those.

Having seen what there is to see, I climb down and I go away, crossing Dartmoor to my home to make some preparations. Out comes a 9 ft 6 in trout rod, a white floating line which will be visible in the dark and an 8-lb tapered leader. Only in the fly does the choice differ from a trout fisher's equipment, and perhaps in the net – you ought to carry a large one, for a grandfather fish may come your way.

Trout men carry many flies, to the extent that the boxes filled with offerings sometimes confuse them and they waste time making up their minds. Not so the fishers of the night, who do not have to match the hatch. Half a dozen patterns cover their needs. If I had to make a choice, I would be happy to fish the season through with just one: a Silver Stoat's Tail tube. But if a change brings hope when all is quiet, try something black: a No 8 Black Lure, or perhaps a shiny fly, a Teal & Silver Blue on which the moonbeams glitter. Just to show that I also suffer such doubts, let me mention a fourth, my own creation, the Burglar, whose dressing will be revealed in Chapter 2. Now there is a fly to relieve the agonies of choice!

The other day I found a flattened stoat on the road, not far from Dartmoor Prison, without a breath in him. Off came his tail, amputated with my pocket knife on a fence post. Two tufts of those fine black hairs, or a contribution from a black labrador, one on each side of a silver-tin-selled tube, have relieved many peal of freedom.

There is a torch in my pocket, midge cream on my face, and the sun has dipped below the hills when I reach the river. With care, noiseless and shadow-like, I creep along the bank to sit beside my tree to wait for the light to go. Robber crows sneak to roost in ivy-entwined trees, and the first of the bats flit by. In the West of Ireland, in county Kerry on the Laune, where Willie is the doyen fisher of the river, they wait until they see three bats before they judge it is dark enough to start. Not being Irish, I cannot tell one bat from another, so that system is no good to me – the third bat to pass might be the first one coming back a second time.

The peal are there, for one or two have leapt – straight up, glistening and shimmering – then the splash and widening waves spread across the pool. The time has come. Picking up my rod and the fly and leader, which have been soaking in a little pool, I cast. Out shoots the line and falls, the fly making a plop in the path of moonlit brightness on the dark, sliding water.

As the fly swims across the river my fingers feel the line for information: a pluck, a pull, some sign. Nothing. Drawing another yard from the reel I make a second cast. Still nothing. Now for the boulder where the great ones lie. A pluck and a mutter of disappointment. The fourth throw is different. The line checks. He leaps and goes for the deep water. We fight it out in the dim light, the rod bent in a fighting arc which curves to a desperate fish. He surges down the far bank, seeking a snag, a tree root or the middle boulder which was his lie. I am full of fear. The pressure tells in time. He gives way and drifts, a bar of light on the mystery of the dark water. Later, as he lies on the grass, thick and strong, scales glistening, I am in two minds: triumph its tinged with sadness.

CHAPTER 1

The Fish

The Seasons

In general, in the British Isles, the sea-trout open season is from mid-March to the end of September. There are exceptions: some rivers start earlier and others do not close until October. Enquiries should be made from the relevant region of the Environmental Agency (EA). A useful source of information on fishing seasons, regulations, EA regional addresses, and available fishings is the biennial publication *Where to Fish* (Thomas Harmsworth Publishing Co).

On my home river, the Dart, the open season for sea-trout is from 15 March to 30 September, both days inclusive. Yet, it is rare for peal to be caught in March, as they have not yet come in from the sea by then. Many rivers in the British Isles do not open for sea-trout fishing by rod until April or even May, and April catches on such waters are usually few. Scottish sea-trout lochs rarely fish well before early July, as runs have only then started to build a noticeable population in the lochs. Then, by the middle of September those lochs, as well the rivers of England and Wales, yield sea-trout of poor quality, for the spawning weeks are approaching. So although the season may open in March and close in mid-autumn, the early and late weeks are rarely worth fishing. It is usually sensible to bring one's fishing to a close not later than 15 September; thereafter the flesh of these fish is soft and not worth eating. On the other hand, in the months of June, July

and August – and May if one is fishing close to the sea – one can have a bonanza.

To understand this one must study the life history of the fish: when it spawns and where; how long it takes to reach maturity; when it migrates to the sea and how often; and the months of return to the river. We will examine these factors in due course, but first I must emphasize the necessity of knowing the fish's life-cycle by showing you when you will have the best chance of a good catch, the reasons will be explained later. The following table shows sea-trout catches on four West Country rivers in different years. I have not included fish whose date of capture is unknown.

The season opens on 1 April on the Camel and the Fowey, and on 15 March, on the Dart and the Taw; all close on 30 September. Why one sea-trout is recorded in March, 1992 for the Camel, and two in 1994 is unclear, as the season had not opened!

Further investigation shows that the April and May catches take place mainly on the lower sections of the rivers, and that by September the fish are congregating in the upper reaches. So it is unwise to book a sea-trout fishing holiday 30 or 40 miles up a river in April or close to the sea in September. In the latter case the majority of fish will have passed through the lower beats before your chosen week.

Why are certain months better than others? The reason is that these fish are migratory: several

RIVER	MAR	APR	MAY	JUN	JUL	AUG	SEP	TOTAL
1991								
Camel	0	0	20	82	237	186	31	556
Dart	2	24	104	41	70	109	95	445
Fowey	0	4	62	67	260	117	55	565
Taw	0	2	16	62	84	82	38	284
1992								
Camel	1	14	12	33	109	158	40	367
Dart	3	20	24	18	109	112	57	343
Fowey	0	9	16	70	367	364	139	965
Taw	2	3	28	27	92	78	91	321
1993								
Camel	0	1	15	60	372	275	124	847
Dart	0	13	33	51	112	180	105	494
Fowey	0	4	57	138	402	155	118	874
Taw	0	3	11	117	195	209	125	660
1994								
Camel	2	0	9	166	498	393	166	1234
Dart	0	54	103	109	309	461	207	1243
Fowey	0	12	45	116	464	235	216	1088
Taw	0	13	51	265	418	301	231	1279

months, or even a year, are spent in the sea, and some time in a river, in which they swim from the mouth to the upper reaches, and back again after spawning. Our task is to catch them as they pass by on their way upstream, and we shall be better equipped to achieve success if we study their life history and behaviour.

The Life-cycle

Sea-trout are migratory brown trout. The two fish have identical structures but differ slightly in colour, the sea-trout being silvery and lacking the red spots of the brown. They also differ in their life-cycles. Both spawn in fresh water – rivers and streams with a clean bed of gravel or small stones. Brown trout remain in fresh water, but sea-trout migrate down to the sea, feed voraciously in salt water, and then return to the river to spawn.

The first stage, spawning, is easily observed. In November I usually walk up a Dartmoor brook connected to the sea by the main river into which it flows. The water needs to be low and clear to observe spawning salmon and sea-trout. The first half of that month is early for salmon, but sea-trout may be seen cutting their redds. A peal redd is a small trough excavated in the clean gravel of the river bed, in the feeder streams or headwaters, by a hen fish. She accomplishes this task just above the tail of a pool, where it shallows and the current, being compressed, increases in speed and washes away any smothering silt. Sometimes the redd is close to the edge of the stream, perhaps conveying a sense of security to the fish. Choice of site is important. If silt covers the gravel, water will not flow through the redd, the ova will be deprived of oxygen, and they will atrophy. Turning on her side she flaps her tail, gravel is dislodged and the current piles it in a small mound to the rear of her position.

The actual spawning involves the hen lying in

Sea-trout and salmon spawn in November and December in this Dartmoor stream.

the redd and quivering in a muscular spasm. This exertion expels ova from the vent. The eggs, being heavier than water, sink into the redd. The cock fish may be with her in the redd or may enter at this stage. He will convulse in a similar fashion to extrude milt (sperm) from his vent. The milt washes over the eggs, which are fertilized. The spawning may take place in a matter of hours or over a day or two. Thereafter, the hen moves forward and stirs the gravel upstream, which washes down to cover the fertilized ova. There are now two things to watch: the ova and the spawned fish, which are known as kelts. First let us follow the development of the eggs.

The time taken for sea-trout eggs to hatch depends upon the temperature of the water – the colder the stream the longer it takes, up to a maximum of about three months. If the water temperature is 5°C the incubation time will be about 90 days; at 6°C it will be about 75 days; and in chalk-stream spring water at 10°C the eggs will hatch in about 35 days. At hatching an alevin emerges. This tiny fish, slightly pink and transparent, has a yolk sac suspended beneath its chin. This food supply lasts for about a month, and when it is exhausted the alevin moves up towards the light from beneath the gravel to become a free-feeding fry and fend for itself in the company of others. By the time it is 2 or 3 inches in length, dark bars, 'finger marks', appear on its flanks and it is known as a parr. It feeds similarly to wild brown troutlets, on shrimp, caddis larvae, snails, nymphs and adult flies taken from the surface of the water – nothing of edible size is safe.

After two or three years, depending on the food supply and thus the rate of growth, the parr reaches a length of between 5 and 6 in. It now becomes silvery in colour, is called a smolt, and in spring swims down the river to the sea.

Although it would be untrue to say that all smolts, after feeding in the sea and gaining weight rapidly to levels between 10 oz and 1 lb, return to the river of their birth in July, August and September of the year in which they migrated to sea, that is certainly the case with the majority. This heavy influx of small sea-trout is the reason for the dramatic increase in the July and August rod catches recorded in the tables given earlier.

These small sea-trout, returning four or five months after going to sea, are known as school peal in the West Country, finnock in Scotland and whitling and herling in other regions. They swim to the headwaters and may spawn in November and December, although some do not. The survivors of this run, known as kelts after spawning, are likely to return to the sea before or after Christmas, feed again, increase in weight to perhaps 1½ or 2½ lb and re-enter the river for the second time during the following spring, summer or autumn, to spawn before midwinter.

This migration to the sea, followed by an upriver journey and spawning, may take place a number of times in a fish's life; the number can be established by looking at the growth marks on its scales (see below). But at all times it is subject to predators, disease, pollution, netting, starvation and other adverse factors, so few spawn more than three times.

Some fish may not follow the normal pattern; instead they stay in the sea for a year or more after migrating as smolts. When they do return they can weigh 1½ lb if they have stayed out for one year, or several pounds if they have been at sea for a long time.

It has been established that sea-trout try to return to the river of their birth to spawn.

Current opinion is that the smell of the river during the initial fresh-water years is imprinted on their brain, so that they can find their parent streams after feeding in the sea.

Their marine journeys may be short or very long. It is likely that school peal which are at sea for four or five months do not travel far beyond the coast. But those which are at sea for longer have been known to travel from the Welsh rivers across to Ireland.

To sum up the effect of the sea-trout's spawning cycles on the weight of individual peal caught by the angler: from March to mid-June all fish are likely to weigh over 1½ lb, since that season's smolts have not yet returned; from July to the end of the season 10–14-oz school peal, the returning April/May smolts of that year, are likely to predominate. Nevertheless, beware of using fine nylon leaders, for heavy fish enter throughout the season.

A Juvenile Electro-survey

Interesting as the spawning scene may be, impressions are inexact in establishing populations, even if redds are counted and compared with previous seasons. Electric fishing may be used to remove unwanted fish from a river, or to rescue valued fish in advance of a pollution making its way downriver. On migratory fish spawning streams it also enables accurate measurements to be made of juvenile salmon, brown and sea-trout, and the adult brown trout population.

I was honoured to be invited by Mike Maslin, the EA River Warden, and Simon Steel, the Senior Fisheries Technician, to watch them survey 65 yards of a Dartmoor spawning brook in June 1993. The operation was timed to take place after all the smolts had run to sea. It was anticipated that the survey would be compared with one to be made in 1996, and thereafter at intervals of three years, to establish the increases or decreases in the numbers of fish.

Salmon juveniles were separated into alevins

Trout, salmon and sea-trout alevins and parr in June, the subjects of a juvenile electro-survey.

an Exeter University graduate. She had already recorded the state of the water before the team went to work: the water temperature was 11.7°C with a low conductivity of 35 microsiemens, both normal for that time of year in a clear moorland stream.

The group worked upstream to allow any stunned fish which had escaped to be carried downstream by the water flow, out of the electric field. The net was also inspected frequently to ensure that tiny fish, which might not be noticed, did not receive more than a few seconds of shock. Caught fish were transferred to a drum of water on the bank, whose oxygen level was maintained by a motorized aerator.

The team covered the 65 yd of brook three times, until almost all fish had been removed. After each pass the catch was identified, after spending a moment or two in a bucket of water treated with a splash of Benzocaine to calm them down. Whilst classifying the fish on a measuring board, Simon said that he is not convinced that anyone can distinguish with absolute certainty between brown and sea-trout fry or parr.

Scale samples were taken from fish over 12 cm in length. Later, Simon sent me the final result of

which had hatched in March and April 1993, and by June had swum up out of the gravel, becoming fry and year-old parr. Trout and sea-trout fry and parr were counted, but they cannot be distinguished one from the other. Nevertheless, a picture could be built of whether trout and sea-trout stocks are altering.

First, 65 yd of the brook were isolated with nets at both ends, the meshes being turned upstream along the river bed and held in place by stones. With power being provided by a petrol-driven electric generator, the negative yellow wires of the cathode were placed in the river at the lower end of the stretch; the positive anode, in the form of a wire hoop on the end of a fibreglass shaft with a safety thumb release switch, was swept from side to side under the water. Simon operated the probe whilst Mike netted out those stunned fish which rose momentarily to the surface and transferred them to water-filled buckets held by Karen,

Juvenile electro-survey. Simon Steel of the Environment Agency classifying young fish which are then returned to the stream

the survey, which revealed an astonishing total of 310 small fish (and two eels!) in 65 yd of a brook about two trout rod-lengths wide. The figures are:

	1st Run	2nd Run	3rd Run	Total
Salmon Fry 0+	66	41	28	135
Salmon Parr ≥1+	40	19	15	74
Trout Fry 0+	32	25	11	68
*Trout ≥1+	23	5	5	33
	161	90	59	310

*These include sea-trout parr

In June 1996 financial considerations allowed only a single run on the same 65 yd of the same brook. The results were:

Salmon Fry 0+	394
Salmon Parr ≥+	51
Trout Fry 0+	30
Trout ≥1+	11
	486

The total of 486 on the run of 1996, compared with 161 on the first run in 1993 confirms that there is a plentiful juvenile stock.

Scale Readings

Unlike salmon and grilse (one-sea-winter salmon), which usually spawn once and then die, sea-trout may migrate from river to sea and then return to spawn several times, swimming down the river to the sea after each visit. The age of the fish at smoltification (the first downstream journey to the sea) varies, as does each marine period. Just as the growth rings that can be seen when a tree trunk is cut through reveal the age of the tree, so the growth rings on a fish's scale reveal its life history.

I do not have the equipment to read fish scales, but I have always been interested in the migrations and spawnings of the fish I have caught. I therefore decided to establish the ages and spawning journeys of the fish taken by my rod on the night of 8/9 August 1993 with the help of the NRA. I removed some scales from the flanks of the five peal which comprised my catch. I packaged them separately and sent them to Kelvin Broad the resident Fisheries Scientist at the NRA, Exeter. The smallest peal would normally have been returned to the river unharmed, but curiosity prevailed. Here are his findings.

8/9 August 1993

FISH A. Weight 0 lb 9 oz. Female, no roe.
REPORT: 20 months old. Gone to sea in May 1993 after one year and about three months in the river. No spawning marks.

FISH B. Weight 0 lb 13 oz. Female with roe.
REPORT: Two-year-old smolt. A school peal. No spawning marks.

FISH C. Weight 2 lb 0 oz. Female, no roe.
REPORT: Two-year-old smolt, spawned once.

FISH D. Weight 2 lb 1 oz. Female with roe.
REPORT: Two-year-old smolt, spawned once.

FISH E. Weight 3 lb 8 oz. Cock with developed milt sacs.
REPORT: Three-year-old smolt, spawned twice, now on third return.

I also submitted scales from two fish caught on the Dart in July 1995 and September 1992 by Luke Chester-Master and Brian Easterbrook respectively.

22 July 1995

FISH F. Weight 5 lb 2 oz. Female with roe
REPORT: River age not determinable due to regenerated scales. It first spawned as a school peal without spending a winter at sea, and had returned to spawn in each subsequent year (three spawning marks in all), and thus on fourth return.

23 September 1992.

FISH G. 10 lb 8 oz. Female with roe.
REPORT: Three-year-old smolt, then spent one winter at sea before returning to spawn in
each of the following four years. Returning for a fifth time when caught. The fish had a
total age of eight years, having hatched in 1984.

The above are examples of peal on first, second, third, fourth and fifth spawning visits, true survivors compared with salmon. As a matter of interest, I have supplied Kelvin with the scales of grilse and salmon weighing between 4½ and 24 lb, none of which had spawned before, and thus were on their first return to the river after one, two or three sea-winters. It was surprising to find that the 24-lb fish was of two sea-winters, whilst a fish of 20 lb had spent three winters at sea.

The Upstream Journey

Even though the sea-trout season was open in March, very few fish are caught in that month. In fact, of all the rivers open in the EA South Western Region, only five sea-trout were recorded in March 1991, eleven in 1992 and none in 1993, apart from eight in one river, the Teign. During that month there is considerable salmon fishing, and large sea-trout, if they were present, would have been just as likely to take a salmon fly or artificial minnow as a salmon in the right water conditions. The fact is that very few sea-trout of any size have entered the river by then. Yet, over the years, my daughter and I have caught large sea-trout many miles above the sea in April and May. In other words, they entered in April and swam steadily upstream, in some cases almost to the spawning areas.

On 1 April 1992, a guest on my beat took a sea-trout of 3 lb, 5 miles above the tide whilst spinning for salmon. It had many sea-lice attached to its flanks. Now, a sea-louse (see photograph 5) drops off the fish after about two or three days in fresh water. The female louse trails egg sacs which drop off even sooner. Yet this peal supported lice with egg sacs, which means it had swum 5 miles in about 24 hours. There is nothing unusual in such an exertion in early spring, if the water is warm. I have taken a number of peal weighing around 4 lb, and my daughter took one of over 7 lb in May, 20 miles above the sea. A friend also took a 9-lb peal, carrying sea-lice, the same distance upstream at the end of that month. Recently, in June, a group of heavy peal, 4- and 5-pounders at a guess, rested for several weeks in an area where many spawn in November. They had made a rapid journey, and now had nothing to do but wait – and avoid me! It is thus apparent that heavy sea-trout run far upstream in a short period early in the season.

As I have said, my water is 5 miles above the sea, and I have often climbed waterside trees in May to peer into the pools through polarized spectacles. I rarely see large sea-trout. It is true that heavy specimens are few in number, but it is my belief that I have missed them because they have run to the middle and upper portions of the river, passing through my water without delay.

In June the scene alters; the movement of peal slows, and 1½- and 2½-pounders, with an occasional big brother, are now the common size, and are seen in little groups of two or three.

By the fourth week of July, one needs an adding machine to tot up the population of a mile of river in the lower or middle reaches of our river in a good season. This is due to two factors: the arrival of school peal, and the slowing down of the pace of upstream movement. In July and August sea-trout of all sizes may stay in a pool in the low or middle reaches for two or three days, and then move on at night in low water to the next holding area, perhaps several hundred yards upstream. By mid-September the fishing has deteriorated in the lower river, as the majority of the run has passed through.

Rainfall, which alters the water height and rate of flow, has a marked effect on the upriver

A first-return school peal (also known as a herling, finnock or shoalie) marked by estuary nets.

journey. Salmon will only run when there is sufficient water to cover the river-bed in shallow stickles to a depth of 3 or 4 ft, and will not jump weirs in early spring unless the river temperature is about 10°C or above. In a small summer river, which may at times be reduced to a trickle, this means they only travel in a spate – the rise and fall of the water level following heavy rainfall in the catchment area. But peal are brave. They will move upstream in both high and low water, but

The square tail of a second-return peal at top. Forked tails of four school peal.

only at night in drought conditions. It never fails to surprise and please me that school peal arrive in July in our water even in a severe drought. Their willingness and ability to swim through shallow stickles, or flap across river-bed stones scarcely covered by water at night is evident from rod-catch figures. Probably the worst recent drought in the West Country was experienced in 1976. In that year the River Dart rod sea-trout catch was 328, just above the average of 312 of the previous four years.

Although peal travel in both high- and low-water conditions, a spate causes increased movement. When one has fished in midsummer for two or three nights in a week or ten days, one gets to know that there is a certain population in the pools, not only from the catch but also from leaping fish. New arrivals replace those that have departed on their journey. Then there is a spate with increased fish movement, which may increase or decrease the population of the pools.

The calendar on my desk tells me when there will be new and full moons, at both of which phases there are spring tides. These high-water influxes into the estuary bring fresh peal, particularly if they coincide with a spate which lifts the level of the river. As my fishing is 5 miles above the sea, a good time to fish is usually two days after the full moon, by which time fresh-run peal will have swum that distance up the river. I do not think the moon and the tide make much difference to the fishing 25 miles from the sea. In fact a full moon may be a disadvantage, as fishing is better on a dark night when the angler is less likely to be seen.

Feeding

Until a young sea-trout, having passed the parr stage, smoltifies and goes to sea, it feeds in the same manner as a wild brown trout. In comparison with the marine supply, river food is scarce. There is a little more to eat in the alkaline chalk streams, but even there there is little available compared with the marine feast. In the acid rivers of the West of England, where spawning conditions are excellent but the supply of food is poor, juvenile populations of brown and sea-trout are considerable, but the size of the fish is small, due to lack of sustenance.

When a sea-trout returns from the sea, it has increased considerably in size and weight, whether it is on a first, second or subsequent migration. The river is now incapable of providing the food necessary to sustain large numbers of fish which may have doubled in weight. And if it cannot sustain them, it clearly cannot provide sufficient nourishment to enable them to increase their weight. The result is that most sea-trout cannot feed in fresh water, but have to live and develop their roe on their own body fat. A fish fresh in from the sea is plump; after spawning it is thin.

There are of course, exceptions; in angling there are always exceptions! Large and small sea-trout, just one or two from time to time, do take individual items of food. This behaviour is more common in those which return to the river in the same year as their first marine excursion and weigh less than 1 lb – the school peal. No doubt their recent river-feeding memories have not entirely faded. I have examined the stomachs of many such small peal, and few, maybe one in five, have eaten something: a nymph, a beetle or a caterpillar. An even smaller proportion, one in a dozen, have foraged with purpose; their stomachs contain a dark mass which, when washed apart in a drop or two of water, are seen to be comprised of nymphs, stonefly creepers, a bee or wasp and other items. The stomachs of larger sea-trout, those on second and subsequent returns, are almost always empty. (See photograph above.)

So why do sea-trout accept our wet flies, dapping flies and spinning baits? It must be said that, on the whole, they do not. Rod fishing, other than with natural bait, is inefficient, and few fish are taken from the total population of prolific rivers. Not many sea-trout are interested

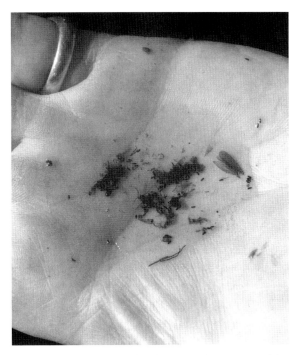

School peal sometimes feed in the river. The contents of this one's stomach were midge pupa, stonefly creepers and an unidentified fly.

in our hit-and-miss activities, unless it is to feel alarmed and swim away. Yet we do catch peal. Large sea-trout occasionally rise from the depths of a Scottish loch to roll over and take down a dapped bumbly fly; all sizes will, from time to time, take a Mepp spoon thrown upstream and reeled back fast in warm summer water; and a sub-surface wet fly in the dark entices large and small members of the tribe to investigate with a frustrating tweak or to take with decision. Why does this happen when, by day in low water, peal seem to rest, comatose, on the river-bed?

There can be no definitive answer. My own view is that memories and excitement stimulate a take. The memory of feeding in the sea or a river may prompt a peal to take a silver-bodied fly as it flickers and moves like a small fish, or a dapped fly because it resembles the mayfly or daddy long legs of its juvenile river seasons. From time to time these flies may stir recollections in the fish's dim, slow minds. The other reason may be an automatic reaction of surprise – the grabbing take as a spinning bait darts downstream across the window of the fish. Think on this: a sea-trout which enters the river in May has to wait until November before spawning. In the intervening months it does not feed; its only task is to swim a few miles up a waterway – it must be bored stiff! It has nothing to do for several months then, suddenly, a Mepp flashes by, and it grabs as at one time it did when on a feeding prowl. These reactions are stimulated by extra water, a spate, a stirring of excitement in itself.

Sight, Hearing and Other Senses

Trout, sea-trout and salmon have binocular vision in an area in front of them, monocular vision to either side, and a blind area to the rear of their bodies.

Their binocular vision warns them of danger ahead, tells them of approaching food and enables them to judge distance. Their monocular vision is mainly of use in alerting them to danger and to food passing to one side; the fish then has to turn to bring its binocular vision into use to judge the take accurately.

On some rivers, and in particular on chalk streams, one is only allowed to use an upstream cast. This cast presents a floating, imitative dry fly, which is carried downstream by the current across the trout's window. The angler is usually casting from behind his quarry and is thus in its blind area. This is not the common approach to sea-trout fishing, particularly at night. Then, a downstream cast is made from a position ahead of the fish, with a subsurface lure or one which floats and drags across the river below the angler. We also cast upstream at night, but casting across, or down and across, the river is more common. We are thus in a visible area and must take care not to be seen. This can be achieved by wading below the bank, cutting one's silhouette by standing in front of a tree, or kneeling on the bank (see page 137).

The deeper the position of a fish, the wider is the window through which he sees the outside world. A trout feeding on floating insects positions himself close to the surface; if he is 6 in down his window has a diameter of 14 in. We know, because we have seen, that sea-trout do not take up such a position 'on the fin', waiting for passing flies; they rest close to the river bed. If a sea-trout is stationary at a depth of 4 ft his window has a diameter of 9 ft. So if we stand on the bank at the river's edge we shall be as visible as a lighthouse against the sky, even at night. You can see this yourself in daylight if you stand on the bank, shielded by a tree, with a shoal of peal in midstream, then move into view. The peal will drift away out of sight into deep water. Whilst I do not believe that at night sea-trout remain in the deep parts of a pool which they usually occupy by day, I have rarely caught them in the dark in water less than 2 ft deep – their window thus remains wide at greater depths.

This means that one must take the greatest care to keep out of sight when fishing for peal, even in the dark. It is well known that sea-trout are easily scared, and their excellent eyesight is one of the reasons. On moonlit nights, fish with the moon shining in your eyes and on your face; never allow yourself to be silhouetted against it. If it is behind you, wade below the river bank. Of course, it would be irrational to suggest that we are as visible at night as we are by day; clearly this is not the case, and it is why this scary fish is more readily caught in the dark. But we are not invisible, even on the darkest nights – fortunately, nor is the fly.

People often ask me how a peal can see a black fly on a dark night. But there is always *some* light, and these fish have a greater ability to make use of it than humans; they have mirror vision. In humans, light passes into the eye through the cornea and then the lens which, by contracting or expanding, focuses it on the retina. From the retina a message of what is seen is carried to the brain by the optic nerve. Excess light is prevented from dazzling the retina by contraction of the iris, which reduces the size of the pupil.

Sea-trout's eyes have a different structure, and they are better able to make use of low levels of light on dark nights. Behind the retina is a mirror, the tapetum, composed of iridocyte cells of silver-coloured guanine. Light enters the eye and is focused by the lens on the retina, through which it passes. The light then hits the mirror and is reflected back to be used a second time by the retina. On bright days too much light would bounce about inside the eyeball, which does not have an iris, if it were not for a sensitive method of control. In high light conditions a dark pigment steals into the silver cells of the tapetum, rendering it ineffective; the pigment fades away as night approaches, allowing the mirror to become operational.

There is a second reason why sea-trout are able to see black flies at night. Usually, the fly is above the fish and is thus seen against the sky – and black is the densest colour.

Sea-trout do not hear sounds made above the surface of the water. One can talk loudly when fishing and still catch fish. The ears of a sea-trout are completely inside the skull, and are mainly concerned with balance and the reception of vibrations. A noise beneath the water surface is probably received, not as sound as we understand the term, but as a vibration. The thump as a care-less angler jumps off a bank onto the sandy river's edge creates vibration waves which are picked up by the fish. If he stumbles in the water a pressure wave crosses the pool. These warning messages are received through the pores which open into canals on the head and along the lateral line on both flanks of the fish. The best way of passing an urgent message to a companion fishing 75 yd away is to shout at him, as this will not disturb fish. You should not run along the bank, boots thumping as you go, to whisper in his ear! Whilst

it is scientifically correct, this advice will not endear you to the opposition concentrating their receptive senses on the far bank! All fishing should be stealthy.

Sensitivity to vibration may also attract sea-trout to your fly. In fast-flowing water a fat fly sets up a greater vibration than a slim lure. When fishing in turbid water after rain, I use a fat tube fly; in clear conditions a slimmer lure such as a single-hooked Black Lure.

Sea-trout can both taste and smell, but to what degree is open to debate. They possess nostrils, tongues and, I am told, taste buds. The current view is that on returning to fresh water from the sea, sea-trout and salmon recognize their parent river by odour. Smell has been used to attract fish since the days of Izaak Walton whose friend, Oliver Henly, anointed his worms with the expressed oil of ivy berries. As Walton wrote:

> He has been observed, both by others and myself, to catch more fish than I, or any other body that has ever gone a-fishing with him, could do, and especially Salmons.

Recently I read in an angling magazine of flies being soaked in ivy-berry oil today which appar-ently made them irresistible.

Sea-trout and salmon are both able to anticipate changes in water conditions before they are apparent to the human eye. Some years ago the Dart suffered a three-month drought which was then broken by rain on the high hills and tors of Dartmoor which form the watershed. Some hours before there was any change in the water level of the lower river two people observed some unusual behaviour by the fish. Salmon which had previ-ously refused to attempt to ascend the fish ladder at the tidal Totnes Weir Pool now made every effort to go up, and fish in one of our pools upstream leapt continuously where they had only jumped before at dawn and dusk during the three-month wait. And I have had many frustrating nights of plucks and pulls at the fly by sea-trout, but no firm takes, just before the arrival of rain. My diary records one such experience on 4 August 1992:

> One peal, 1 lb 14 oz. 1-in Silver Stoat's Tail tube. Had four more splashy pulls in Embankment Glide and and Monk's Pool, where I momentarily hooked a large peal or grilse which departed in a boil of water. I think the peal were playing about with the fly as rain was on the way. Continuous rain arrived later in the night.

Identifying Sea-Trout

A few large sea-trout start to enter some rivers in March, at a time when their season may not have opened. Some of these peal weigh as much as two sea-winter salmon, for which anglers may legally fish on some rivers in March. Moreover the salmon season sometimes continues throughout October and even into December, whilst on most rivers sea-trout fishing ceases on 30 September, as on the Camel and the Fowey. So a large sea-trout may be killed out of season in November in the belief that it is a grilse; such rivers are the Camel and Fowey. On the other hand in Dorset, on the rivers Frome and Piddle, salmon fishing closes on 30 September, whilst the sea-trout season remains open until 31 October.

In the few cases where the weights of the two fish may be similar and the seasons are not identical, it is necessary to distinguish between them to avoid breaking the law by not returning to the river the out-of-season fish. The problem does not often arise with any fish weighing less than 3 lb, for grilse are rarely that light – 3½ lb is about their minimum – and, in any case, are not in the river until late spring or early summer. An experienced angler will usually be able to tell at a glance whether a 5-lb fish is a salmon or a sea-trout, but a novice needs to examine structural details. Once in the early 1970s I was staying at the Rising Sun at Umberleigh in early March, before

Sea-lice on the tail of a sea-trout.

the sea-trout season had opened on the river Taw, and a novice fisherman brought in three fish, none of which weighed less than 7 lb, yet one was a peal!

There are several ways to tell the difference. First there is the **tail**. The trailing edge will be straight or slightly convex in a heavy sea-trout, while the tail of a salmon or grilse has a concave trailing edge. (The tail of school peal and finnock is forked.)

There is also a difference in the **eyes**. With the mouth closed, the hindmost edge of a sea-trout's eye is forward of the rear end of the maxillary; in salmon, it is level with and vertically above it. The head of a salmon is also somewhat pointed, particularly in cock fish, while the head of a sea-trout has a stubby appearance.

If you count a line of **scales** from the rear of the adipose fin down to the lateral line, you will find that there are 13–16 scales on a sea-trout and 9–12 on a salmon. When you have had some experience studying the two fish you will also notice that the scales of a sea-trout are smaller than those of a salmon of the same size. One day, in a summer spate, I took a medium-sized sea-trout on a salmon fly in a place where I often take

Distinguishing large sea-trout from salmon and grilse:

a. The sea-trout's eye is forward of the end of the maxillary.

b. The rear edge of a salmon's eye is in line with the end of the maxillary.

c. Sea-trout on the second and subsequent returns from the sea have a straight end to the tail. It is forked on small sea-trout on first return (see photograph of net-marked school peal).

d. Salmon and grilse tails are concave. There are usually between and 12 scales in a line down from the rear of the adipose fin (by the large daisy) to the lateral line. Count them on this photograph. Sea-trout have 13–16 scales.

salmon and grilse. In the middle of that month grilse are likely to be in the region of 4 lb, whilst September entrants to the river from the sea may weigh 5½–6 lb. Identification was confirmed by a scale count noted in my diary:

> 14 July 1993. The Flats. 3 lb 10 oz. 1¼-in Black Dart tube. Water coloured, medium height. Took as soon as the fly hit the water. This peal had 16 scales from adipose to lateral line. Rose a salmon in tail of BP and had a pull from another in the Saucepan.

Gill maggots are often found in salmon which have been in fresh water for some weeks, but they are not found in sea-trout. (It is sometimes said that gill maggots are only found in salmon kelts, but this is not correct from my own observations.) Sea-lice are found on both fish on entry to the river from salt water. Indeed, so heavily infested are some finnock on the west coast of Scotland that these small first-return sea-trout often die. This sea-louse plague is said to be due to an explosion in the louse population arising from the siting of numerous salmon farms close to the river estuaries.

Finally, there are usually more black **spots** on the flanks of sea-trout than on salmon, although this is not a reliable method of identification.

CHAPTER 2

Night Fly-fishing Tackle

An accomplished trout fly-fisher, whether on river or stillwater, is likely to possess the main items needed for night fishing – a rod and a reel. It is in the specialized equipment, such as nets, torches, flies and fly lines that he may need advice. Nevertheless, in this chapter I will cover everything needed for an ideal outfit.

The Rod

A friend of mine once caught a 10½-lb peal on a 9-ft trout rod at night. The fish fought with such power that its leaps resulted in such loud crashes onto the water surface that a nearby angler thought my friend had fallen in. The fish had to be stranded on a sandbank, as the available nets were too small. But the 9-ft rod did the trick after a prolonged battle. So if you can fish with a rod of that length without fatigue, and it is comfortable and has the capacity to cover the water, then you should not be ambitious and over-taxing your physique with a longer one. The 5 lb 2 oz peal mentioned in Chapter 1 was caught on a 9-ft Normark Gold Medallion trout rod which is well suited to dry-fly fishing with a No 18 Black Gnat and leader tapered to a 3-lb point.

Personally, I fish with a 9 ft 6 in rod, but there is no ideal length which will suit all people and all situations. Some rivers are narrow, others are wide, there are heavy sea-trout, and 12 oz school peal and finnock. A rod for fly-fishing in a river at night must be a compromise to some extent.

Until recently my night rod was a carbon-fibre 9-ft AFTM (Association of Fishing Tackle Manufacturers) No 7/8 Hardy Farnborough No 1. This rod was designed for distance casting wet flies and lures on stillwater, where it is still part of my equipment. It is on the stiff side, throws a narrow loop of line at high speed and is thus excellent for cutting into the wind and for dealing with substantial fish. The common size of peal in my river is in the 2–3-lb range up to the end of June, and after that school peal predominate. At any time of the season one may connect with a brave 4-pounder. The rod was unsympathetic to little fish, but controlled large peal with authority. Broadly speaking, it coped with all situations where the hooks of my flies

A 9-ft Hardy Farnborough No 1 AFTM No 7/8, with push-in butt extension and Dragonfly 100 reel.

were strong singles, or Partridge No 10 outpoint X1 or X3 trebles in my tube flies. Several seasons ago I started to fish regularly in low- and medium-water conditions with my new fly the Night Prowler. There is nothing original in using a flying treble hook in a sea-trout fly, but the Prowler treble is tiny – No 16 – and the mouth of a fresh sea-trout is soft. A stiff rod can, and does from time to time, tear the hook free from its hold. Sometimes one or more of the three hooks on the treble opened slightly under the pressure applied by the stiff Farnborough rod, and the fish swam free.

To counter this risk, I needed a rod of easier action, one which would bend to the savage take late in the night when I was dreaming in the dark, and accommodate the startling leap of a 3-pound fish under the far bank. The Normark 9 ft 6 in AFTM No 7/8 two-piece Alcedo carbon-fibre fly rod with ceramic guides is moderately priced in relation to its quality and capability. No rod would look better at twice the price, and I am certain that the performance would not be much better. My Alcedo casts well, handles fish and sees that they are landed, and one cannot ask for more – indeed, it is the rod used by the successful members of the international Kingfishers Team Normark.

There are 9½-ft Alcedos available with easier actions at AFTM 5/6 and 6/7. I like the No 7/8 earlier in the season because one needs the power to handle large sea-trout and the occasional salmon. When school peal arrive one might go to the No 6/7, which would also be a very good dry-fly river trout rod. 10-ft models are also available in two or three pieces; the extra length makes them suitable for fishing from a boat.

For young anglers, ladies of willowy construction and men of light build, a 9-ft rod would best suit their physique. Indeed, my daughter takes all her peal on a No 6/7 rod 8½ ft long – a tough little weapon on which she does all her river trout fishing. The 9-ft Gold Medallion I mentioned earlier has now been superseded by the 9-ft

A 10 ft 6 in Bruce & Walker Salmon & Sea-Trout rod. AFTM No 7–9, screw-in butt extension and Hardy St John reel.

AFTM No 6/7 Cortland HT and the more expensive Cortland Golden Eagle. These rods are a delight to use at a wide range of fish: little moorland brown trout, stocked rainbow trout in lakes and lazy trout in luscious chalk streams.

At the top of the power ladder, I have sometimes lifted down from my rod racks a 10 ft 6 in AFTM No 7/9 Bruce & Walker tubular carbon salmon and sea-trout rod with a matt finish to the tube instead of glossy, flashing varnish. This weapon was christened on a 3¾ lb peal on the first night I took it to the river. Its length and strength enabled me to wear down the fish whilst standing thigh deep in mid-river in a strong water flow. A factor in favour of a long rod is the amount of line it can keep out of the water when one is playing a fish. A 3-lb peal usually makes an initial fast upstream run which may take out 25 yd of line, and then leaps a couple of times when it comes to a halt. Those leaps put considerable strain on the hook hold if much of the fly line is on or under the water surface. A 10 ft 6 in rod holds much of this line above the river. But, by the time I had been casting for a couple of hours it seemed as though the rod demanded excessive effort in relation to my strength, my wrist ached, and I was glad to pack up and go home. That rod is really an ideal single-handed salmon fly rod for use in small, overgrown rivers. Because false casts are rarely made, salmon casting is much less physically demanding than wet- or dry-fly fishing for trout or sea-trout, where false casting is usually necessary.

So a 9-ft AFTM No 6/7 proved too light for me, and a 10 ft 6 in AFTM No 7/9 too heavy; the 9 ft 6 in rod established itself as my regular nighttime companion. My general advice is to suit your physique but choose 9 ft or longer in order to gain a fraction more power than would be normal for a river trout rod.

I should say a word about butt extensions. These usually have a spigot which slides – or screws if it is made of metal – into the rod behind the reel mounting on the butt. They are 2–4 in in length, and act as a brace to the rod hand when pressed into the stomach whilst playing a heavy fish, particularly a salmon. They also keep the reel clear of the braking effect of one's clothes – a valuable consideration with exposed rim fly reels. The 2-in length is ideal, either as an optional extension which may be fitted when desired, or as a permanent built-on feature. The 4-in extension seems to me to be too long; it sometimes catches the fly line which is to be shot when false casting in the dark.

Modern carbon rods need the minimum of maintenance, but it is wise to examine the silk wrappings of the line guides each winter and add a coat of varnish if necessary. Whether the rod has a spigot junction at the centre of a two-piece model or a female socket to the top section and male end to the butt section, it is wise to rub a wax candle over the 2 or 3 in that are pressed into the top section of the rod. This prevents wear, and helps to stop the joint loosening whilst casting. With all rods it is sensible, every hour or two, to check that the joint is not working loose. The female socket in the top section of a rod is likely to split if the butt section works loose, providing a sloppy fit, and you can often continue casting without noticing the problem. The first

sign of such a condition is usually that the line guides become out of line on the two or three sections of the rod.

A rod should not be put away in the rod bag whilst wet. I take my rod to and from the river made up on rod clips on the roof of the car. When they are not in use, I rest all rods horizontally on 13-ft home-made rod racks, their tubes supported at 1-ft intervals on wooden dowel pegs. If you do not have a rack, the rod should be hung vertically behind a cupboard door or in a similar out-of-the-way place in its cloth bag. The tape cloth ties should not be tightly wrapped and knotted around the rod – the sections are not going to escape! – as tightly wrapped rods may become warped if they are made of split cane.

The Fly Line

The AFTM Scale of Line Weights is based on the weight of the first 30 ft of the fly line, excluding the 1-ft level tip. It thus includes the tapered portion of both double-tapered (DT) and weight-forward (WF) lines and some of the thicker belly of the DT line and of the thinner centre section of the WF line, both of which are likely to have a total length of 25 m or 27 m. The DT line is tapered at both ends and is therefore reversible when the first end wears out. The WF line is not reversible. The tapered sections of both types of line are likely to be between 8–12 ft in length. The scale runs from No 4 (light trout rods) to No 11 (15- or 16-ft salmon rods).

The AFTM rating of a fly rod is based upon the supposition that the average angler false casts 30 ft of line outside the rod tip before making the final delivery and perhaps shooting 1 or 2 yd of additional line. The lines in use on sea-trout rods

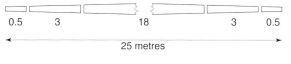

| 0.5 | 3 | | 18 | | 3 | 0.5 |

25 metres

DOUBLE TAPERED FLY LINE

are likely to be within the range No 6 (light) to No 8 (medium). In selecting the weight of line to use for night sea-trout fishing, we must take into account the distance we need to cast. This is because in a narrow river we may false cast less than 30 ft of line outside the rod tip. Thus, if the rod is rated No 6 there would be an insufficient weight of a No 6 line outside the tip to balance the action of the rod, which would be underloaded. In such a position it would be better to use a No 7 line on the No 6 rod. The converse is also true, although it is unlikely to apply at night: if one habitually false casts more than 30 ft outside the rod tip the line should be lighter than suggested for the rod by the manufacturer. For those starting fly-fishing, who may not false cast 30 ft, it is advisable to use a line one classification heavier than that suggested by the rod maker.

Most of the sea-trout I have caught at night have been at an average range of 10 yd, but as I shoot the final 2 yd the false cast length is only in the region of 8 yd or 24 ft. If my rod is rated No 7 it would be underloaded with a No 7 line and I therefore use a No 8 line. So to sum up, for short casting at night one should use a line heavier by one category than that suggested for the rod by the manufacturer.

Line profiles vary: there are double-tapered (DT), weight-forward (WF) and shooting-taper or shooting-head (ST) lines. The WF and ST lines are mainly used in open conditions on lakes or wide rivers by day for distance casting. For night fishing it is best to use a DT line. My choice for short casting with the 9 ft 6 in Alcedo rated at No 7/8 is thus a double-tapered No 8 floater (DT8F). The 'F' in the designation indicates that the line floats. And it will not float better if greased – in fact, floatants applied to floating lines may damage the coating, causing the plastic cover over the braided core to crack, let in water and sink. The practice of greasing fly lines is a hangover from the years up to about 1960, when lines were made of silk and had to be greased to float. In the early years of my fly-fishing career it

was bad practice to make up one's rod, greased line, leader and fly and carry the outfit to the river on the roof of one's car. The greased line would rub against the leader, which could not then be made to sink. But today fly lines are plastic coated, with a braided core of Dacron. They are rot-proof and thus do not have to be dried after each excursion to the river, as was the case with silk lines.

Whether fly lines float or sink depends on whether they are lighter or heavier than water. Those which sink do so at varying rates, depending upon their densities. There are also sink-tip lines (F/S) in which the first 8 or 10 ft sinks whilst the main belly floats, and they are available at varying densities to sink slowly or rapidly. The place of these lines in the tackle bag has largely been taken recently by braided leader butts of varying densities. These will be discussed in the section below on leaders.

Whilst it is clear that there is a place for a sinking line in some rivers and at some hours of the night, I fish mainly with a floating line. This is because in my river, in those places where peal take up station in the dark, the water is not deep. A sinking fly line would cause the fly to catch on the bed of the river, and there would be the same result with a sink-tip. It has been said that a sinking line should be used in the early hours of the morning when fish activity is reduced and peal 'go down'. There may be value in this advice if the water is suitably deep, but when that time arrives my shoulders are usually aching, I have a fish or two in the bag and bed seems more attractive than floundering around in a depressingly lifeless river.

Over the years I have caught trout, sea-trout and salmon by day using fly lines which have been coloured white, ice blue, light green and mahogany. Gradually all but the light green have been discarded. Watch someone casting with a white or ice-blue line – it flashes in the sky, and when this happens over water, trout may be seen to dive for cover. The camouflage of mahogany, a 'blend with nature' colour, attracted me, but I have discarded it, as it is almost impossible to see on the river surface when I am salmon fishing in tawny-coloured spate water, and thus did not point to the position of the subsurface fly.

All this changes at night. White is then the colour, or else a very light blue or green. It is hard enough fishing in the dark without the added problem of being unable to discern the path of the fly as it swings across the river in the current. A white line draws one's eye to the lure, and points out the underwater position of a hooked fish. Go for a white line on dark water. The only exception to this choice is in bright moonlight; it is then better to revert to the light green line you use by day.

One further point. Buy a line which has a smooth surface and thus will shoot smoothly through the line guides of the rod. Test the surface by running it between the fingers of your hand. It need not be an expensive line, but it usually rules out the cheapest ones, which are sometimes so rough that they can be heard grating through the rod rings and are almost impossible to shoot any distance.

The lines I have used over the years include the floating, smooth-surfaced, double-tapered, light green AirCel by Scientific Anglers, and the AirCel Supreme floater, also by Scientific Anglers, which is white, expensive, and excellent. Another good white line is the Cortland 333, which is in the medium price range and costs slightly more than the green AirCel.

The Fly Reel and Backing Line

The modern trend by manufacturers towards wide reel drums, widened at the expense of reduced diameter, does not attract me. A small diameter of 3¼ in, no matter what the capacity is, does not look right on a 9 ft 6 in rod. It look's like a man's rod saddled with a boy's reel. It was once said, more than 50 years ago, that if an aeroplane looked right it flew well. I believe the same applies to reels. My inexpensive 3¾-in Dragonfly 100 carbon reel has been in use, night and day, since the marque came on the market many years ago. Nothing has gone wrong, no part has failed, and if it is a little more finger-polished than when first it felt the touch of raindrops, that is surely a sign that I have been well served. This reel is still manufactured in its original form by popular demand, after being taken off the market for a short time.

The Dragonfly Concept is the latest additional version made in Cornwall by British Fly Reels Ltd in three sizes, and supplied with two spare spools. The 395 model, the largest, is right for a DT8F line and 75 yd of 20-lb monofilament backing. This is also the capacity of the original 100 model. Both reels have adjustable disc drag and an exposed rim for additional finger braking.

It is pleasant to be able to fish at night with a silent reel, but at times it is necessary to create a noisy click to warn an angler arriving on the far bank of one's presence. It is all very well standing in mid-river, ethereal and undetected by man and fish, but the effect is marred if the opposition on the other side wraps his flies about your neck. Warn him off with a twirl of the clicking ratchet.

There are so many excellent reels on the market that I cannot describe more than a small selection. I will confine myself to two more at the top and bottom ends of the price range. There is no doubt that the House of Hardy makes reels of superb quality, and it is only to be expected that perfection carries a price to match. Take a look at their catalogue, obtainable from the Pall Mall shop and from Farlow's of Pall Mall, and inspect their 3⅝-in Marquis 8/9 and Marquis 3¾-in No 8 disc drag, which can be adjusted to silent use.

At the other end of the price range and yet entirely reliable in my experience is the Leeda RimFly which is made in four sizes, again by British Fly Reels Ltd. A RimFly Kingsize 100 will take a DT8F line and 75 yd of 20-lb monofilament backing. It is not silent, but has adjustable drag and exposed rim for finger braking.

Beneath the fly line there should be sufficient backing to nearly fill the spool. If the spool is not filled almost to capacity the handle will have to be turned a greater number of times to recover a given length of line. The required length of backing may be established by first winding the fly line onto the reel, then filling it almost to capacity with the backing. Then pull it off and reverse it. The backing also provides a reserve of line if a heavy fish runs away downstream and should not be less than 75 yd when sea-trout fishing. Do not forget that you cannot run after a fish in the night.

Two types of backing are available: braided and monofilament. For a number of reasons I prefer monofilament of 20-lb breaking strain. It can be joined to the fly line with a needle knot, which runs out smoothly through the line guides of the rod. Braided backing cannot be inserted into the end of the fly line to form a needle knot, and the more bulky Albright knot has to be used, or a nail knot which, although slim, is not as fine as the needle knot. Both Albright and nail knots might snag in the angle of a snake-pattern line guide. Braided backing, when drowned beneath the surface by a distant hooked fish which has pulled off a lot of line, creates greater drag on the hook hold than smoother monofilament. Finally, it takes up more room on the reel spool, which thus accommodates a shorter length. Backing of both types should be attached to the reel by an Arbor knot.

Leaders

A leader for night sea-trout fishing ought not to be long or it will form too great an almost weightless proportion of the line/leader combination outside the rod tip, and the rod will be insufficiently flexed. If the rod is 9 ft 6 in long, a suitable leader for night use is between 8 ft and 8 ft 6 in, and thus, as an additional benefit, the line/leader junction will be outside the rod tip when you net a fish on the surface of the river.

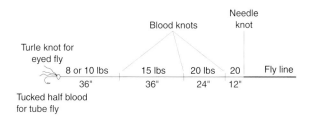

When salmon fishing, one is almost always casting downstream; the current then straightens any curls in the leader after a less than straight delivery of the fly. Casting to sea-trout, one may be throwing upstream, downstream or across, and with or against the wind. Good turnover of the leader is essential to ensure that the fly alights at the extremity, and starts to swim and fish at once. Moreover, knots may be created if the leader falls in coils and loops. To achieve straight turnover a tapered leader is essential. My leaders are home-made for subsurface lures, and are in three sections: the butt – 2 ft of 20-lb Maxima Chameleon monofilament of 0.018 in diameter; the middle – 3 ft of 15-lb Maxima Chameleon of 0.015 in diameter; and the point – 3 ft of 10-lb Maxima Chameleon of 0.012 in diameter or, in clear low water, 8 lb of 0.011 in. This combination produces an 8 ft leader. The butt is then joined by a blood knot to between 6 in and 1 ft of the same 20-lb Maxima which is attached to the point of the fly line by a needle knot. The short portion needle-knotted into the fly line starts at a length of 1 ft, but by the time the leader has been replaced a few times this length is reduced to about 6 in, at which point it is replaced.

The line/leader junction in this arrangement may be reeled smoothly through the rod tip ring without becoming stuck when netting a fish on a short rod. With a 9 ft 6 in rod the junction is unlikely to enter the rod tip ring as the leader is 1 ft shorter than the rod. This precaution is essential at night for one cannot see the joint in the dark to keep it out of the rod tip. The same almost level union may be achieved with a braided loop connector. These are 6-in braided nylon sleeves with a small loop at the end to which a blood bight loop tied on the end of the leader is attached, loop to loop. The point of the fly line is inserted 4 in into the hollow sleeve, and is held in position by what Orvis describe as the "Chinese finger cuff" grip. In effect, the harder the loop is pulled, the tighter the braided sleeve grips the fly line. A short plastic tube about 1 in long, supplied with the connector, slips over the braid to cover the end, which is now 4 in up the fly line, and stops the sleeve unravelling. This tube may be held permanently in position by a spot of superglue or a single drop of Fishin' Glue. If the braided loop system is chosen, the butt of the home-made leader should be increased to 2 ft 6 in to form a total length of 8 ft 6 in. In my opinion, braided loops are a poor alternative to the needle knot, which is the smoothest and safest line/leader junction.

Another method of creating suitable and versatile leaders is with Airflo braided leaders of differing densities and thus sinking speeds. These have a loop attachment to the fly line, and are 4–5 ft in length. A tippet of about 4 ft of 8- or 10-lb Maxima is then knotted to the point of the Airflo braid with a water knot. These braids control the depth at which the fly swims beneath the surface when fished off a floating line, depending upon whether one uses intermediate, slow-sink, or fast-sink braid.

Always take the greatest care when fishing sub-surface lures that the nylon does not skate on the surface of the river. If it does, each of the junction knots will create a small wake to frighten a timid peal. This risk is automatically overcome with a slow-sinking or neutral braid, but home-made leaders require treatment with sink-mix, which is prepared as follows.

Buy a 100-g carton of Fuller's earth from the chemist, and borrow the washing-up liquid from the kitchen sink. Take a small piece of cloth and dampen it under the tap. Sprinkle the cloth with Fuller's earth on both sides and add a dozen drops of the washing-up liquid. Squeeze it until it is impregnated and then store it in a 35-mm film-spool container. Wiped over a nylon leader it will cause the monofilament to sink beneath the surface at the first cast. Proprietory products which achieve the same result are also available, such as Mucilin Quick Sink, and Ledasink. And if none of these are available, a little mud wiped over the leader will have a similar effect, although repeated use of mud scratches the nylon, making the leader more visible to fish.

For floating, wake-creating lures of a bushy, dapping fly type, cast down and across to produce a 'V' upon the river surface, I prefer a Leeda knot-less tapered leader. This should be of a 9-lb breaking strain which is the 0X classification. The 3 or 4 ft of monofilament butt closest to the fly line, being the thickest part, should be greased, but the point length should be left ungreased or even rubbed over with sink-mix.

Sink-mix materials, wet cloth and 35mm film case.

Subsurface Flies

My first expedition for sea-trout was on a boat on a Scottish loch, by day, in the early 1950s. Not knowing much about the business in hand, I followed the instructions of Murdo Campbell, the boatman. It can be a crushing experience having the contents of one's fly box scrutinized by a horny-handed Highland gillie whose dialectal utterances are, sometimes intentionally at other times fortunately, incomprehensible. In this case, his opinion was clear: if a sea-trout was caught on one of the flies clipped in those neat rows, it would be one more than he expected. Having much pride in the success of his boat, Murdo withdrew a rusty tobacco tin from his pocket. Inside was a jumble of small scruffy wet flies on No 10 or No 12 hooks, all hooked together, their tattered feathers witness to their popularity with the sea-trout of his loch. Grouse & Claret, Black Pennell, Peter Ross and others of that style were prised apart and knotted to our gut casts, and proved irresistible. We caught sea-trout. From 10 oz to 7 lb they surged up, and engulfed those little rusty-hooked lures.

This daylight success with small traditional wet flies led to many disappointing nights in my subsequent river-angling career. Unlike loch flies, lures for night fishing should be long and slim. Singles ought to be dressed on No 6 or No 8 lure hooks, and many of my 1-in socketed tube flies are 2-in overall when the treble hook and over-lapping dressing are included. This does not mean that long flies should always be used; in low, clear water, particularly if it is warm, the length may be reduced. But it does mean that, on average, flies for use in the dark are better attractors if they are above the size of daylight offerings.

We have seen that sea-trout have efficient night vision, and also that they are sensitive to vibration. It is a matter of conjecture whether a barely detectable water disturbance alerts a peal to the presence of the lure, but I believe it does. A dog's sense of smell, an owl's huge eyes in rela-tion to the volume of its skull, and the asymetric positions of its ears, the ability of an insect to attract a mate from far away, are all examples of sensitivities of which we have little appreciation. The faintest underwater undulations in the current arising from a fat tube fly held against the flow may alert a sea-trout to the presence of your lure in turbid water. On nights of heavier than normal flow, as a spate recedes, I fish my fat tube flies.

Some anglers fish more than one fly at night, adding a dropper halfway up the leader. There is no doubt that this adds to the risk of creating tangles, some of which necessitate wading to the bank, which causes a disturbance. The trebles of a tube fly can catch in the meshes of the net when taking a fish, so how much will our problems be increased by a second fly, which we cannot see in the dark?

So it is one fly at night for me, and for a novice let that fly be single-hooked. The treble of a tube tangles more frequently on the nylon leader than a single hook, even when the tube is socketed to retain the eye of the treble. If socketed tubes are not available, the treble may be kept in line with the tube by attaching the leader to the hook eye with a *tight* seven-turn tucked half blood knot. This long knot is drawn up into the fine hole in the tail of the tube.

The beginner should stick to two patterns, and thus avoid the agonies of too much choice: a black fly for dark nights and a blue and silver lure for lighter situations. And have faith in your offering. If these two flies do not take a fish there is probably something else wrong, not the fly – your casting may be splashy, the air may be colder than the water, the fish may be able to see you sil-houetted against the sky, you may be wading clumsily, or the fish may just not be there. Here are these two patterns:

Black Lure

Hook: Partridge Code 01 Single Wilson No 8
Body: Black floss

Rib: No 14 oval silver tinsel
Throat: Black cock hackle
Wing: Two black cock hackles
Silk: Black Naples

Teal and Silver
Hook: Partridge Code 01 Single Wilson No 8
Body: Flat silver tinsel, ribbed fine oval silver wire
Wing: Teal flank feathers
Silk: Black Naples

After you have gained some experience, add tube flies to the armoury.

Alexandra tube
This fly is about 2 in long overall if measured from the head to the ends of the peacock herl; it is also fat and creates a disturbance. It is for use in stained water and fuller flows.

Tube: 1-in Veniard Type B Slipstream socketed
Hook: The No 12 Partridge CS8 black outpoint treble is designed for sea-trout. It has a large eye to aid knot tying in the dark, and the long shank of ⁹⁄₁₆ in extends beyond the dressing to catch the 'tail nippers'. If it is unavailable, a Partridge X1 black No. 10 outpoint treble is a good substitute.
Tag: Scarlet floss
Body: Flat silver tinsel
Wing: Peacock herl
Head: Black varnish
Silk: Black Naples

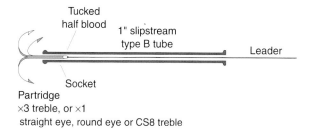

ALEXANDRA AND SILVER STOAT'S TAIL TUBE FLIES

Silver Stoat's Tail
This is shorter than the Alexandra, as the length is limited by the short hairs of the tail of a stoat. It is more durable that the Alexandra, the peacock herls of which are inclined to break off. Never pass a dead stoat on the road; casualties are my source of supply. Amputate their tails on a roadside fence post with your pocket knife and then wash your fingers in a puddle. This fly produces enviable results! But stoats' tails are in short supply, so a good substitute is bucktail dyed black.

Tube: As in Alexandra
Hook: As in Alexandra
Body: Flat silver tinsel
Wing: Two tufts of stoat's tail, one on each side, to reach at least the end of the tube
Head: Black varnish
Silk: Black Naples

Now I come to two special flies with which one may be very confident of attracting and landing fish. Their names are my own.

The Burglar
To make this all-black fly, take a long-shanked No 6 streamer hook, such as the Partridge bronze down eye D4A, with the hook cut off at the bend, leaving just the shank and the eye. To the rear of this you are going to attach a Partridge Code XI black No 10 outpoint treble hook. (It is actually easier to cut off the hook at the top of the bend *after* you have completed the dressing. The bend and point can then be held in the vice until you have finished.)

Using 15-lb monofilament, attach the treble behind the end of the streamer shank, leaving a gap of ¼ in. In this arrangement it is not possible for the shank to lever out the hook. Take the treble, loop the nylon around the back and pass each end through the eye from opposite sides. Whip the nylon down onto the treble shank with black Naples silk. Whip the two strands together

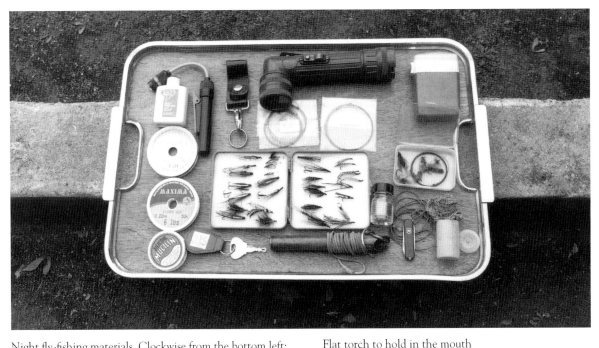

Night fly-fishing materials. Clockwise from the bottom left:

    Mucilin floatant for wake lures
    Maxima Chameleon nylon for leader tippets, 6 lb and 8lb
    Jungle Formula insect repellant
    Swan-necked torch
    Hang-all belt-loop
    Red-filtered torch, beneath which are spare leaders and a
       fly box
    Flat torch to hold in the mouth
    Surface wake lures
    Sink-mix
    Swiss Army scissors on a cord to go around the neck
    Supafloat for wake lures
    Priest on a cord to go around the neck
    Spare car key
    Centre: Subsurface lures
    Home-made leaders

just above the treble eye. Now, leaving the ¼-in gap between the cut-off streamer shank end and the treble eye, lay one strand along the shank and cut off behind the hook eye. Pass the other strand along the shank and through the streamer eye, turn back along the shank, and then whip down both strands onto the streamer shank. The mount is now formed and should be varnished, as should the silk wrapping the treble shank. The dressing is very plain: rib the body with flat silver tinsel to protect the silk, and tie in a long wing of bucktail dyed black.

The key to the success of the Burglar is the flexible mounting of the treble hook, as there is no possibility of a long shank levering out the treble.

The Night Prowler

I designed this fly in the mid-1980s, but gave up using it because whenever a peal was netted, one of the hooks on the treble, or the main single, penetrated the fibres of the net mesh. As this usually entailed wading ashore to free the hooks, much frustration resulted. Two years ago, after some fruitless and frustrating nibbles by cautious peal, the Prowler was given another swim. All went well, provided the fish was picked off the surface of the water by hand. If the net has to be used with a large fish, you can reduce the chance of the hook penetrating the meshes by varnishing the bag of the net.

The prime feature of this fly is the No 16

Partridge CS8 black flying treble. This is whipped to nylon behind the short shank Code A No 8 Albert Partridge Wide Gape down-eye single hook. The combination must be made up before the fly can be dressed.

Place the single hook in the vice and roughen the shank with sandpaper. Varnish the shank.

Take the treble, pass 12 lb nylon monofilament through the eye and around the back, and pass each strand back through the eye in opposite directions. Whip the nylon strands onto the treble shank in the same manner as for the Burglar.

This nylon is finer than the 15 lb used for the Burglar as there is more dressing to be applied to this pattern and the result has to be kept as slim as possible. Moreover, the treble is smaller. Offer the treble up to the single hook, with its eye level with the single's bend. Attach the flying treble in the same way as for the Burglar but with the Wide Gape hook intact. There are thus four hook points to the completed fly. A flexible gap of ¼ in should be allowed between the eye of the treble and the rear of the whipping on the shank of the single hook.

Body: Flat silver tinsel on single shank, red paint on shank of the treble
Wing: Six strands of peacock herl to extend just beyond the treble
Cheeks: Two short jungle cock feathers
Head: Black varnish
Silk: Black Naples

Surface Flies

The night-time dry fly is not really a fly at all, it is a floating object capable of producing a 'V' wake when held on the surface against the current or pulled downstream faster than the water flow.

Black Muddler

As good a surface lure as any is a well-greased Black Muddler, preferably with a fatter head of deer body hair than is usual for an underwater trout lure. The deer body hair is spun on at the head to surround the hook. On a subsurface Muddler the head is trimmed at the front, and wider at the back. To create a wake, the head should not fine down behind the eye of the hook.

Hook: Partridge D5B Long Mayfly No 8
Body: Black floss silk
Rib: No 14 oval silver tinsel
Wing: Squirrel tail dyed black
Head: Body hair of a red deer
Silk: Black Naples

Tony Allen Bucktail Mayfly

Deer hair is naturally buoyant, as each hair has a hollow centre. This mayfly, dancing downstream at dusk on the water surface, attracts peal. Tony dressed some samples for me to use at mayfly time for trout on the Test and the Kennet. Having a few left over in my box I allowed myself the naughty pleasure of a dragging mayfly when I was after peal. They worked, but the heavy hand of authority would descend upon my shoulder if I were to use them downstream on a chalk river where, rightly, no dragging is the rule because it is not the natural action of a fly – and it is too successful!

Hook: Partridge D5B Long Mayfly No 8
Body: Yellow seal's fur ribbed fine gold wire
Front hackle: Blue dun
Palmered hackle: Blue dun
Tail: Three ginger cock whisks
Wing: Brown natural bucktail. Split shaving brush tying.
Silk: Yellow gossamer

Miscellaneous Equipment

Two fly boxes are needed: one for subsurface lures and the other for surface wake lures. For sub-surface lures use the Leeda pocket-size fly box. It is a floating plastic box 4½ in square and hinged on one side. It comes in red, yellow or blue, costs very little, and is supplied with two loose white self-adhesive plastazote liners. Peel off the backing of the liners to reveal a sticky surface, and then press them down firmly inside the lid and base. If bulky flies are to be carried, only one surface should be lined. This is a most useful box which used to be supplied free with the medium-priced Leeda Hi-Tec Galion fly line. Being slim, it fits into one of the front pockets of a fishing waistcoat, and the flies are clearly visible by torchlight against the white foam lining. I have used no other box for several seasons. A wide range of flat etha foam boxes is also available, and they are particularly suitable for tube flies; the treble can be squashed into the foam.

Surface lures must not be squashed, and should not be hooked into a flat surface or the fly will be flattened on one side. Place them in a white Saxa ground pepper container, the 25-g size. A 35-mm film container is also is suitable, but rather small. Before placing surface lures in this simple box soak the Mayfly in Supafloat, and grease the Muddler with Mucilin. Do this at home so that grease is not transferred on your fingers to the leader, causing it to float.

It is as well to ensure that the surface lure holder is a different colour from the sink-mix cassette. The 35-mm film cases are usually black, grey or white, the grey, or black may be chosen. A more reliable way of selecting the correct container when rummaging in one's pockets in the dark is through size; a Saxa container is much larger than a film case.

I will consider the **net**, **fish bag** and **belt clip** together, as they all hang from my belt whilst I am wading. The key to the suspension system is an Orvis Hang All belt loop which has a brass spring clip on which I permanently place an extra 1½ in split ring.

Next to my right thigh I hang the fish bag, the peal can be slipped inside after being knocked on the head by the priest. The House of Hardy sell trout-sized washable fish bags, which can be suspended by a split ring threaded through the handles. This ring is clipped onto the Orvis belt loop. Another suitable bag is a plasticized cloth grocery shopping bag produced by Sainsbury's, which is in a suitably dull brown colour. The heavy plastic bag I use advertises Heineken lager, and another advertises *The Evening Standard*. Do not trust traditional woven reed bass bags, they rot after repeated submersion and drying, with the result that peal may slide out through a hole in one corner and slip unseen into the river.

My net has a metal 20-in bowframe and a 20-in non-telescopic hinged handle. I use the handle as

The Evening Standard fish bag suspended beneath the 20-in bowframe net on a Hang-All Belt Loop.

a wading probe in the dark, and I know that the water will shortly flood over the tops of my thigh boots if my hand becomes submerged. The frame is slightly smaller than is safe for large peal, although it has accommodated 5-pounders. A 22-in frame, such as the Pelican Grilse DeLuxe 55, is better. It has a silver-coloured frame which is visible against dark water and is thus outlined when netting fish.

A net in the Gye sliding handle design is not suitable for night use unless you place it open on the bank beside you. Whilst the 24-in Gye is superb for salmon, you cannot easily release the peal sling strap holding a 20- or 22-in sea-trout Gye on your back, pull out the handle, net the fish and then replace it on your back whilst wading.

Do not use nets with Y-shaped folding arms; they sometimes fail to open if the ends of the folded arms become caught in the net meshes. The cord joining the extended arms may also sag under the weight of a fish balanced between them, allowing it to slide back into the water.

The spring clip on my net shaft is hung on the extra split ring of my belt loop, and is outside the fish bag. It is a simple matter to lift off the net when a peal is played out, flick the frame open, net the fish as it rests on the surface, knock it on the head and slip it into the bag. And it can all be done without moving my feet and causing disturbance by leaving the river.

The **priest** and **scissors** are suspended on cords around my neck. The scissors are of the Swiss Wenger army type, red in colour, and have a lanyard attachment. They are essential, when replacing point sections of leaders, to trim off nylon ends, and to trim the half blood knot of tube flies and the Turle knot used for eyed single-hooked lures. They should hang mid-chest.

The priest is on a cord of sufficient length to allow it to be stored in my right trouser pocket and to allow sufficient slack to hit a fish on the head. Priests are available in brass, plastic, weighted staghorn and other materials, and the

prices vary enormously. I use a 6-in length of ½-in iron steam pipe with a split ring at one end. My daughter carries a field-gate latch with a hole at one end through which a bolt once passed, the bolt having been replaced by the cord. A small spanner is also suitable.

Care and accuracy are needed in the dark when you are holding a peal in your left hand and hitting it on the head with the priest gripped in your right. Pained mutterings are sometimes heard on our river as I miss the fish and hit the knuckle of my left index finger, which is now permanently swollen.

Be particular about your **torches**, and carry three. The reason for this is as follows. To guide you between pools, when crossing stiles and fences, and when dealing with tackle problems in the field beside the river, a flat torch is best. This takes a 1289 battery and can be held between your teeth, leaving your hands free to undo knots or tie them and make up tackle. Its size and shape also make it easy to store in a waistcoat pocket.

But such a torch is not suitable for use in the river as it might drop into the water, and the bright light will scare the fish. That is why I carry two others with me. They enable me to unhook the peal and change flies whilst wading, although I always turn my back to the area to which I am

The author's priest is a piece of metal pipe. Lara Bingham uses a gate latch. A priest should be secured against dropping in the river by a cord around the angler's neck.

The author's torches.

casting before I turn them on. The smaller of the two has a flexible swan neck and a clothes-peg-type clip which is attached to the collar of my sweater beneath my chin, where it remains throughout the expedition. Its two LR6 batteries provide enough light to change a fly.

More substantial is a green ex-WD type DT-109/5 torch in which the reflector head is at right angles to the cylinder body. It takes two D size batteries. In the base are a spare bulb and a set of coloured filters. If the red filter is fitted, your night vision will not be impaired nor, I believe, will the fish be disturbed. On the back of the torch is a spring clip which I fit to the centre of my belt; the light is thus level with my hands when I am dealing with the fish. It is as well to carry this torch in a pocket until it is required. If it is clipped to your belt when you raise a leg to climb out of the river up a bank, your thigh may push up the clip and free the torch, which could drop into the river. Another useful light is the adjustable Petzl torch mounted on a head harness (see photograph).

After taking considerable care with sink-mix to ensure that your leader does not show on the water surface, the effect may be spoilt if you put greasy **midge cream** on your hands, and so transfer some to the leader. Boots market Dual Action Insect Repellant Gel, which is not greasy, and the pump-spray Jungle Formula is also an effective deterrent. Do not forget the midge treatment, or you may be forced from the river. When you are changing a fly by torchlight on the bank, you will find that midges home in on the beam, if they are not already doing their best to obtain a free meal from untreated wrists, ears and the back of your neck.

Supafloat, made to the late Richard Walker's formula, is an efficient liquid **floatant** for the surface lure mayfly. To waterproof the Black Muddler, immerse it in Supafloat, allow it to dry, then grease the deer hair head with solid Mucilin. This should be done at home before going to the river.

Now we come to **waders and clothes**. Whether you wear gumboots, thigh boots or chest waders

Petzl lamp, ref E04700 with 4.5v battery. The lamp is adjustable for elevation.

Above: Close-up of the quick release clip, and the cord which is looped around the neck and under one arm.

Right: The author's wading staff with lead weight and rubber button at the bottom.

depends on the water you are fishing. Thigh boots suit my home river, but not the type that has heavy metal studs, which make a noise on the rocky riverbed. Cleated composite soles are quiet in use and safe enough on a sandy bed, but they do not grip well on slippery surfaces. A felt sole is silent and rarely slides, but the felt sometimes becomes detached from the boot. My own thigh boots, 4 in longer in the leg than most makes, are Ocean studded, but the studs are tiny, only just protruding from the sole to give a firm grip. And they do not wear out before the boots, which are themselves long-lived.

Chest waders are hot and heavy for long-distance walking. There is not much to be said for them when fishing for peal in rivers of little depth, other than that they enable one to sit down on a dew-laden bank to eat one's supper.

Wear dark clothes at night. Sea-trout fishing is usually done in the warm months of June, July and August when, even in the small hours, a sweater provides sufficient comfort over a cotton shirt and vest. I wear a dark green pullover, a fishing waistcoat and dark olive corduroy trousers. The fishing waistcoat is an ideal garment. Well endowed with pockets, it leaves my arms unencumbered for casting and keeps me cool on muggy nights – usually the best weather for sea-trout. If you wear a hat or cap to keep the insects out of your hair, wear a dark one.

All these garments and waders are available from Farlow's of Pall Mall, London SW 1.

I do not use a **wading staff** on my home water, as I know the riverbed well, having inspected it frequently. On a strange beat it would be unwise to wade without a staff to probe ahead in the dark and steady oneself in uneven places. My own staff is home-made from a 50-in length of stout ash cut from an overgrown hedge. After drying it in a shed for a year, I soaked the bottom 6 in for 24 hours in wood preserving liquid. Then I pressed on 12 oz of old lead pipe with a 2-in bore, such as was used in old houses, just above the base. The base is protected and made silent by a rubber cap such as those used on invalid and other walking-sticks. The handle end is in the 'Y' form of a thumb-stick, and I loop a loose cord over one shoulder. On this is a clip which can be attached to a metal ring encircling the staff 6 in below the thumb grip. The staff then hangs, leaded end submerged in the river whilst I am fishing, but can also be left to one side on land simply by detaching the clip on the cord from the metal ring on the staff.

Do not wade at night unless you have surveyed the river by day, and do not wade at all unless you can swim. If you fall in, or if a gravel bank shifts under your feet or an overhanging bank collapses under your weight, do not throw your arms up in the air in panic. Instead, roll onto your back and kick with your legs towards calm water, meantime paddling with your hands. Waders full of water will not cause you to sink, but they will be heavy when you scramble out onto a bank. So roll out, then raise your legs to let the water pour out of the waders. The Register of Experienced Fly Fishing Instructors, Schools and Guides issues a leaflet on safety to all pupils. The Secretary, Richard Slocock, will send a copy on receipt of a stamped addressed envelope. His address is: Wessex Fly Fishing, Tolpuddle, Dorchester, Dorset.

Various **buoyancy aids and lifejackets** are available in the form of fishing waistcoats which can be inflated by CO_2 bottles, foam-padded waistcoats, and lifejackets which will turn an unconscious person over, keep the head up, and automatically inflate. Leeda market the Automatic and the Manual Crewsaver, both of which are activated by a 33-g CO_2 bottle. The Manual is activated by pulling a red 'jerk to inflate' toggle, and the Automatic activates when it is immersed. The House of Hardy supply automatic lifejackets which double as fishing waistcoats with numerous pockets. Some Hardy models also act as short waterproof wading jackets. It is important that CO_2 lifejackets are worn outside all clothing; if they are covered, they may not have room to inflate.

The difference between lifejackets and buoyancy aids should be understood. A lifejacket will turn you over and keep your head out of the water, even if you lapse into unconsciousness. A buoyancy aid just helps a conscious person who is able to swim.

CHAPTER 3

Night Fly-Fishing Tactics

If I can pass on to you my own enthusiasm for night sea-trout fishing, my purpose will have been achieved. The fascination of scarcely perceived midnight mysteries will involve you in an endless attempt to solve the problems of catching sea-trout at night. Why do non-feeding peal take the fly? Is it better to fish on dark or light nights? What parts are played by the moon, thunderstorms, river mist and drizzle? Anyone wanting to catch peal, will try to address these problems and, in so doing, move some way towards perfecting his approach – but only some way, because none of us succeeds consistently, which is just as well, for satiation kills appetite.

There are a number of factors which will contribute to your success – or otherwise.

The Month

You have to be dedicated to fish the early months of April and May at night. Sea-trout are present in smaller numbers than later in the season, but those in the river are heavy fish of superb quality. I do not start regular night fishing until June, but that is a personal choice based on the comfort of warm nights and on the fact that there are few residents or fish of passage in my beat in April and May. Other anglers, devoted to their sport, are out in the dark in those early months close to the sea, and particularly in tidal waters. On average, May produces five times as many rod catches as April, and one third of the number taken in June.

We catch sea-trout of substantial size on our beat in April and May, but only by chance, when salmon fishing in a spate by day.

The end of the third week in June brings the shortest night of the year. Darkness hardly falls, particularly if there is a full moon. One is rarely able to start casting a fly before 10.45 pm or go to bed before 3.00 am – that is if you want to have fish on the kitchen draining board for all to see at breakfast. But although June is demanding of stamina, it rewards us with peal of substantial weight; almost all are over 2 lb.

My favourite night-fishing weeks are in late July and throughout August. There are sea-trout of all sizes in the river: many school peal of 10–14 oz (the smallest should be returned) or even 1 lb in weight; fish of 1½–3½ lb on their second or third river visits from the sea, and one or two heavyweights of 4 lb and above, full of experience and power. This is my diary entry for 4 August 1991.

> Sea trout three. Best 1 lb 13 oz. Fly – the Night Prowler. Best fish beyond last tree at top of Embankment Glide. Two school peal in Concrete Post. Had a number of plucks and flurries in CP – all came off an Alexandra Tube. So, when a bat got hooked I took the opportunity to change the fly. Released bat. Put on the Prowler. Had four takes, took three peal.

Fish on their third and fourth spawning runs are still entering from the sea, and continue to do so until the middle of September. It only takes them two or three days or, in a spate, a few hours to reach our beat 5 miles above the sea. An even shorter time may be taken to swim through the ¾ mile of our water and thus, as the runs tail off in September, our population diminishes as fish speed upstream towards the spawning areas in short spate periods of full flow.

So early and mid-August are the choicest times for both fish and the advancement of dusk. By the end of the month one can start at 9.00 pm on cloudy nights, and have two or three fish in the bag by midnight. Night fishing for peal is more tiring than going for trout or salmon by day, as one is constantly concerned with maintaining one's balance. And getting to bed by midnight is more appealing than the late night required when fishing in June.

In some years September is productive, but fish are only in reasonable condition close to the sea. Even there, the roe will be in the later stages of development. If they are caught a long way up the river late in the season, their flesh is likely to be soft, not worth eating, and they should be left alone. There may be a late entry of numerous school peal in early September, owing to a delayed departure from the river as smolts in April and May of the same year due to drought. I recorded in my diary for 6 September 1990:

> Two peal. 1 lb and 1 lb 7 oz. 1-in Alexandra Tube and No 8 Black Lure. A good number of peal have appeared. A late entry possibly due to late departure of smolts to sea by reason of this year's spring drought. Brian Parker 1 lb in tail of the Manse. Self, 1 lb 7 oz in tail of Embankment Pool. Tony had a peal of 2½ lb previous night. Full moon. I saw a female hen harrier glide across the road.

In an earlier season, again after drought throughout the summer, the bag for two friends and myself was six peal on 5 September and 12 (including three brown trout) on 7 September. The heaviest of these fish was 3 lb 6 oz, but the majority were schoolies.

The drought/late entry theory is supported by the fact that in mid-May 1996 smolts of about 5 oz were still present in the spawning areas of Dartmoor after a late, cold spring with very low rainfall. I caught them in the River Swincombe and the Blackbrook on dry fly and a 2-lb point whilst after brown trout. It is wise to fish those waters at all times with barbless flies, or press in the barb with snipe-nosed pliers. Try not to touch salmon parr and smolts, but release them underwater. If they must be held to facilitate hook removal, be sure your hands are wet and cold.

Water Conditions

In spate rivers holding salmon and sea-trout in summer one has a chance either at salmon by day or at sea-trout by night, sometimes both, if you can stand the strain. Salmon fish well as a spate starts to fall, and then activity tails off as the final extra inches of water run away. Sea-trout, on the other hand, are not so obliging when a full river starts to drop from the immediate peak, but chances increase from the time the spate has dropped about two thirds of the way back to low summer level. As the days of spate fishing are usually fewer than the nights when the river is at a low level, August might provide four days of good salmon fishing from two spates in a small river, and two dozen nights of sea-trout fishing. Naturally, some of those nights will be better than others.

Lack of rain brings salmon fishing almost to a standstill in small rivers, unless by worm, shrimp or prawn, or in a stable chalk stream fed by springs. One of the worst drought years this century was 1976. In that season in the 18 recorded rivers of the south-west of England, the salmon catch was reduced from an average of 3,168 fish for the four years 1972–75 to 1,809. The sea-trout take only dropped from 7,856 to 5,668, which is within the normal margin to be expected from one season to another.

It can hardly be disputed that peal fishing is

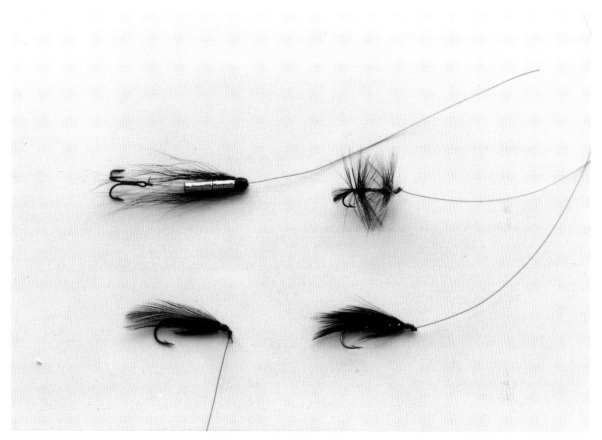

The treble hook of the Silver Stoat's Tail tube fly is knotted to the leader with a tucked half blood knot and then drawn into the socket at the tail of the tube. The dapping fly and the two Black Lures should be kept in line with the leader by the two-turn Turle knot. The Black Lure below the tube fly has been incorrectly attached by a tucked half blood knot, allowing the leader to move freely around the eye and the fly to fish at right angles.

rewarding in low water, but even better in the two or three evenings as the river settles back after a flush. In low clear water I tend to use small flies; in coloured conditions a long fat tube is better. This is not only because of the increased chance of a large lure being seen, but may be because it causes attention through vibrations or disturbance of the steady flow of the current.

Sometimes a spate will bring down dirty water and be slow to clear after a long dry spell. It is then necessary to make a decision on whether sea-trout can see the fly in the stained or thickened flow. To test the chances before daylight has departed, wade in to a depth at which the water level reaches 6 in above your knees. If you can see your feet the water is sufficiently clear for fish to detect a 1-in tube fly. I apply the same test when I am fishing for salmon.

After mid-May do not bother too much about water temperature and its effect on the depth at which the fly should be worked. Following the middle of that month my fishing is done entirely with a floating line because my water is not deep in the best peal lies. A friend who fishes a deep pool on a chalk river uses only a fast-sinking fly line, which also counteracts the strong lifting current. In those places where the pool shallows, he moves the fly at a faster rate of retrieve to keep it from snagging the riverbed. If you are fishing before mid-May, on cold nights, it would be sensible to try a sink-tip line if the water depth allows.

Whilst you need pay little attention to water temperature in summer as a guide to the depth of fishing the fly, a hot and prolonged summer drought reduces fish activity – although not to the extent that it is not worth making an expedition. Warm water does not eliminate one's chances, but they are reduced. And air temperature in relation to water temperature is very important, as we will see.

The Weather

Much sleep can be unnecessarily lost fishing on nights when adverse weather conditions put down the fish. Although clear, dry moonlit nights are conducive to romance, it is damp, cloudy, warm nights when midges are about that are best for sea-trout fishing. A clement drizzle is ideal.

The night of 17 July 1987 fell during the period of peak school-peal runs. It was also a warm night of clouds and abundant insect life, evident when midges swarmed about my head, and bats hawked flies over the river. Here is my diary entry for that night.

> Five peal. Total 6 lb 1 oz. Best 2 lb 1 oz. Black Lure No 8 and 1-in Alexandra Tube. With Brian and Tony. Four in tail of the Manse, one in tail of Embankment Pool. Lost two or three, including one being played by Tony whilst I photographed. Removed the tail of a stoat found squashed on moorland road with my pocket knife – will make good silver Stoat's Tail tubes. On the way back a roe deer jumped out of the road over granite wall into prison field. Many bats about on the river on warm cloudy night. Sea-trout caught 10.30 pm to

12.30 am. Brian lost a gilse in the Manse on No 4 U/S [upstream cast] Mepp Aglia in the morning.

On the subject of stoats' tails, you would do well to befriend a skilled tunnel-trap keeper on a Hampshire pheasant or partridge shoot. Stoats of the chalk downs, like trout of the chalk streams, must feed well. On my desk are two richly aromatic tails, each 6 in long, and eight more await collection from a farm near Andover. The hairs are almost long enough for Collie Dog salmon flies! In return for these gifts, which my wife fails to appreciate in the house, I collect the skulls of sheep which have succumbed to the rigours of Dartmoor winters. Their short horns are in demand for the handles of thumb sticks.

I like a drizzle, but heavy rain makes conditions miserable and usually unproductive. Not only is heavy rain itself unproductive, the hours before a downpour are likely to be frustrating. On such nights one is plagued by peal plucking at and tweaking the fly without being hooked (unless one is using the Night Prowler).

> 9 August 1988. Two school peal. Total 2 lb. 1-in Alexandra Tube. Tail of the Manse; top of Embankment Pool. Many plucks and pulls. I believe the tweakings take place when rain is on the way. Confirmed next day by many hours of wet weather.

and on 4 August 1992 I recorded a 1-lb peal and the following experience:

> Had four more splashy pulls in the Manse and Embankment Pool where I momentarily hooked a large peal or grilse. This fish departed in a boil of water. I think peal were playing about with the fly as rain was on the way. Continuous rain arrived later in the night.

Wind at night does not help one catch fish, as it does during the day on a sea-trout loch by roughing up the water surface. A cold wind is not helpful, and if the air is colder than the water, poor results are to be expected. If my hands become cold when I am fishing whilst wading on a chilly night, I sometimes dip them in the river to test the water temperature. If the river feels as warm as milk fresh from the cow, then sport will be poor, as the air is colder than the water. Mind you, one ought not to be discouraged from an outing if there is a stiff breeze on a summer evening, for the wind often dies at dusk. But a cold wind which arrives in the night will put down fish.

> 24 July 1993. With Walter. Three school peal on Silver Stoat and Alex tubes as soon as we started at 10.45 pm when air warm, then cold north wind arrived to shut down activity.

Do not be put off by mist. Sometimes you will see a white bank of mist rolling towards your position, it may soon swirl between you and the opposite bank. Continue fishing; the air may clear as rapidly as it thickened. If it does not, the chances are reduced.

> 20 July 1994. The Burglar. 13-oz brown trout, 15-oz school peal, 1 lb 9 oz peal. CT pool. Two nights before full moon. Cloudless night. When mist came over the water the fish went down. I think there was an otter in the tail of the pool.

> 1 September 1993. Three peal, best 1 lb 9 oz. Silver Stoat tube with No 12 Partridge CS8 treble. Full moon, clear sky. Took fish 9.30 pm to 11.00 pm. Mist came up later, and came and went from time to time, still caught fish. When mist became permanent and night grew cold, activity ceased. Saw fox and badger on way home.

Thunderstorms are a different matter – go home. It is dangerous to fish in such conditions with your own personal lightning conductor, in the form of a carbon-fibre rod – or any other rod. It is even risky to pick up the rod to walk back to the car whilst lightning flashes in the sky. I put my rod down in such a storm, turn up my coat collar,

hunch my shoulders and wait for the flickers and rain to move away, for fishing can be spectacular after a storm. But it seems that thunderstorms take longer to pass than they used to, so it is better to go home to bed.

The Moon

The phases of the moon should be studied for two reasons. Full and new moons result in high spring tides flooding into the estuary, which may bring in extra sea-trout. And in the river the extra light provided by a full moon can make fishing difficult to the extent that some anglers prefer not to fish, for peal are scared by incautious movements in high light.

First let us consider spring tides. The extra runs of fish up from the estuary are only likely to be noticeable in the lower reaches. Once sea-trout are spread over several miles the effect of a spring tide is barely noticeable unless there is a spate at the same time to urge them through several miles of the valley. If your beat is 3 or 4 miles from the sea, a distance that a peal may cover in two or three days, or less, good fishing will be experienced 48 or 72 hours after the full moon.

> 31 July 1988. Four peal, total 3 lbs 12 oz. 1-in Alexandra Tube. Two days after full moon, with river on the high side. Took photographs of Ben and Chloe [my dogs] with the fish.

Now to the actual fishing. A full moon in a cloudless sky does not stop one catching sea-trout but it does mean that one has to be careful not to scare the fish. It may also cause a rapid cooling of the air to the extent that this becomes colder than the water, resulting in little reward for your effort.

If you are fishing in a full moon be sure you are not silhouetted against the sky. Although moonlight reflected off the water may dazzle your eyes, it is better to fish with the moon in your face than outlining your head, body and rod from behind. In bright moonlight, you would be well advised to wade, for your low position will reduce your silhouette. It is safer to fish whilst wading below a bank than kneeling on it or – to be avoided at all costs – standing on a bank above the water. It is almost impossible to cast from behind a bush at night, and inadvisable to position yourself in front of a tree to cut the silhouette. In that position you cannot extend an overhead back-cast and be forced to use a roll cast. To sum up, catches can be good in bright moonlight if one makes stealth the key to success.

Whilst bright moonlight has both advantages and disadvantages, I like a strong moon hidden behind clouds, for this provides a diffused light and also keeps the air warm.

> 9 August 1992. Five school peal. No 8 Alexandra single hook with flying treble and jungle cock cheeks. Three-quarter moon behind clouds. Warm. No wind. Midges. Peacock herl cut short at back of treble hook to reduce fly in low water. Those fish which took whilst I was casting across the current were all hooked and landed. Failed to hook some which plucked directly downstream. Picked fish out by hand whilst wading to save treble catching in net meshes, knocked on head, dropped in bag at waist. Three had roe; one milt. All stomachs empty. One 10 oz returned.

A full or three-quarter moon behind clouds provides a diffuse mellow light. There is enough to see the fish move, to handle tackle and the coffee flask without a torch, and to avoid falling over a slumbering cow.

Many anglers prefer the darkest nights when there is no moon. Certainly, there is less risk of frightening the fish with one's silhouette, or the flashing in the sky of a light-coloured fly line. Of course, June and early July nights are never really dark; one can always discern a white line on dark water. On 19 June 1990 I christened a new 10 ft 6 in Salmon & Sea-Trout rod by Bruce & Walker.

> One peal. 3 lbs 12 oz. 1-in Alexandra tube. Right in the tail of the Manse. Moonless. Low water

after a little rain. Fly dressed by Lara [my daughter]. One savage take. A great fighter which leapt with a crash under the far bank. Before dusk saw a hobby flash along the river after swallows or house martins.

Daylight Reconnaissance

Searching the river by day to establish the presence of peal in the pools is an enjoyable and necessary task. The knowledge that fish are present increases one's confidence, and one's determination to catch them.

The ability to see peal is a knack that has to be acquired. One has to know where to look, what one is looking for – grey shadows and their sun shadow on the river bed – and develop the knack of looking into, rather than at, water. It is necessary to be circumspect in approaching the river, for a peal which sees a peering human outlined against the sky will melt away to hide in a deep place. There lies the difficulty – the availability of deep hidey-holes in areas shaded by trees.

I make my approach to the water's edge using the trunk of a tree for cover. I then climb the tree koala-fashion from behind. Once in the branches, shielded by leaves, I can see a great deal. I can watch and estimate their sizes and their condition – sea-trout are not always free of disease. If you cannot see any fish, do not descend at once. Wait and watch. It is difficult to make out the inhabitants of the deep half of a pool from the shallow side whilst fish remain stationary, but peal can be frisky! Frequently, whilst observing a shoal, you will see a fish twist on its side with a flash of silver flank. This movement is usually accompanied by a short tour of the water within a 20–30 ft radius of the shoal. It then returns to its original position. Many times a pool has appeared unpopulated until a silver flash reveals an almost invisible shoal of inhabitants.

Do not always expect to see peal facing upstream. They must face into the current in order to breathe but, in back eddies, this may mean they have to point towards the sea. There is such a place in one of my pools where, almost under my feet by day, undisturbed sea-trout rest in shallow water. Sometimes there are as many as ten or 12 together. I have never caught one there at night, which raises another point – sea-trout move about after dark. This is not so much a problem as it might appear because if one consistently fishes a stretch of water, one soon gathers some knowledge of favoured night-time haunts.

In general, in my experience, sea-trout move from deep to shallower lies soon after dusk. This view is supported by my catches, and by the fact that peal do not need the cover of deep water after dark. Certainly, fish are taken regularly in a 2-ft depth in the tail of one of my pools just before the water breaks into the next stickle, whereas there is never a peal there by day.

Having said that peal move from deep to shallow water with the arrival of night, I have found that they often remain in the areas they occupy by day if it is of medium depth. In one place in my pool Embankment Glide there is a boulder one third of the width of the river from my bank. I sometimes waded out to this stone in order to cast under the far bank. On climbing a tree one sunny day, I could see a line of peal in front of the stone, like ships in line ahead at a naval review. There is no doubt that these fish, or more accurately their predecessors, must have been disturbed by my wading. On the next visit at night I covered this lie by casting upstream whilst standing beneath my bank and stripping back the fly. The reward was a 2 lb 4 oz peal. I then felt free to wade to the stone to cast to the far side.

In addition to establishing the whereabouts of fish, the daylight inspection is essential for safety reasons and to establish what casting techniques will be required in the dark. I do not use a wading staff at night in my river because my feet know every hole, ledge and boulder. On a strange river one should use a staff, and wade the pools by day to establish which are the safe and which the

dangerous areas. The survey also clarifies whether it is necessary to cast over your right or your left shoulder, where to beach fish or wade ashore, how high to keep the back cast, and the safe length of the forward throw.

When I am teaching people to fish at night I am often asked how to estimate the maximum length of cast before catching the fly on the far bank. The problem is easily resolved in moonlight – you can see the pitch of the fly as it plops upon the water. If a dark night is in prospect my practice on a strange water is to go by day to the place from which I am to cast. Then I count the number of arms-length pulls of line from the reel needed to cover the lie. When I return in the dark, I withdraw this amount of line, and that represents the required distance. Other anglers knot a cotton thread around the line at intervals of 3 or 4 yd to establish the length of line off the reel and outside the rod tip. For me, the actual weight of line false cast in the air is sufficient indication of the length of each throw. Sometimes I misjudge and the fly hooks onto a tree branch overhanging the river from the far bank. When this happens, I can only pull and break it. To wade across in the hope of releasing the fly would disturb the river and might take me over the tops of my thigh boots.

Casting in the Dark

It is a mistake to try to learn to cast from a book, however well endowed it may be with photographs and diagrams. Go to a qualified casting instructor – there is information on how to find one at the back of this book.

In the discussion which follows, I have assumed that you are capable of a plain overhead cast, the most commonly needed style. Sometimes a steeple cast, which is a development of the overhead, is needed to lift the line above bushes behind you.

At night in a river it is rarely necessary to cast a long line. You should concentrate on delicacy and avoiding tangles. The further one casts the

A wrist support keeps the back cast up above the bank behind when wading. Available from Sportfish.

less control one has over these. Delicate delivery is the product of good style and practice. Tangles are usually caused by the fly catching on the line/leader junction, or by a wind knot. They are not entirely avoidable, but they can be kept to a minimum. To avoid the fly catching on the line or leader an elipse should be formed in the overhead cast. This means that if you are casting right-handed over your right shoulder, you should take the back cast away slightly to the right, and bring the forward cast back straight overhead. If you are casting with your right hand over your left shoulder, possibly to avoid a tree to the right, you should take the back cast away to the left and bring the forward throw back overhead. With these precautions the fly rarely becomes tangled.

Even so, frequent checks must be made to ensure that all is well, there are no wind knots, and the treble of a tube fly does not have the leader nylon looped over one of the three hooks.

There are two things to do to check whether the fly and leader are in the original state. The first is to cast your fly on a short line onto an avenue of light on the water. If you look about you when wading, you will find that there is almost always a light area on the river where the sky is reflected. Cast upon this to see the fly plop down at the extremity of the leader. This is the most frequent check. The second is to run your fingers down the leader to check for wind knots and to feel the fly. It is no use trying to take hold of the leader with the rod held up in the air and searching for the leader with a waving hand, for you may well catch the fly in your sleeve. Instead, draw in the line with rod horizontal until just 1 ft remains outside the rod tip – this is easily visible with a white line. Now, hold the middle of the rod with your right hand, run your left along to the tip and grasp the fly line outside the top ring of the rod. The rod hand can now be slid back to the butt and the left hand down the leader to the fly (see photograph below).

If there is a tangle do not wade ashore unless it is absolutely necessary. Unless the problem is complex it is better to turn your back on the peal area and, with the pencil torch at your neck and the red filter light at your waist, sort out the muddle in mid-river.

Preparation at Home

Few of us live within walking distance of a river. The majority have to prepare and gather together their tackle at home, transporting the equipment to the fishing by car. This section ensures that you do not arrive at the water without everything you need or with inadequately prepared tackle. It is better to set up an outfit in the afternoon than

To find the fly in the dark and check for wind knots, run your hand down the line and then the leader. (*Tony Allen*)

struggle to make up leaders, waterproof surface lures and so on in the dark.

Choose your rod for the night for subsurface lure fishing, attach the reel, run the white floating fly line through the guides and knot your home-made three-section leader to the 1-ft length of 20-lb Maxima nylon. This short length should be needle-knotted into the end of the fly line. If you have prepared your leader with a loop at the end of the butt section this should be joined to the fly line via a braided loop. Attach a suitable fly (which can easily be changed if the water condition on arrival is not as you anticipated it would be). The fly can then be hooked to the keeper ring and the line reeled up, and the rod is ready to be transported to the river on the rod clips on the roof of the car.

If you intend to fish a surface wake lure as well, dip several flies in Supafloat and allow them to dry. In addition to this treatment smear the lures with solid Mucilin. Take a second rod, reel, white floating line, Leeda knotless tapered OX leader and waterproofed fly, and set up this outfit before also placing it on the car roof rod clips. Immediately before leaving home anti-midge your face, neck, ears, wrists and hands. A single treatment lasts for many hours, and this advance application saves carrying one more item to the river. It also allows any stickiness to wear off your hands before you start to fish, when you might transfer some midge treatment to the leader, causing it to float.

Now check the other tackle you will need. If the night is fine it is sufficient to wear a fishing waistcoat over a thick, dark sweater. Put some of the tackle items into the waistcoat pockets before leaving home. Here are some checklists:

In the waistcoat pockets
- flat torch for finding your way across the fields and over stiles
- flat red Leeda fly box containing subsurface lures
- Saxa pepper container holding prepared surface lures
- Supafloat and solid Mucilin
- sink mix in 35-mm film case

- spare home-made and Leeda knotless tapered leaders
- 50-m spools of 10- and 8-lb Maxima Chameleon nylon for leader points
- white plastic carrier bag in back pocket to hold fish placed upon the bank

On your person
- priest, looped on a cord about your neck, and stored in your trouser pocket
- scissors, looped on a cord about your neck, hanging at chest level
- net and fish bag on Orvis Hang-All Belt Loop
- ex-WD red filter torch on centre of trouser belt
- swan-necked torch clipped to sweater neck beneath your chin
- thigh boots
- pocket knife
- hat or cap to keep midges out of your hair

In a game bag to be left at a convenient place beside the river
- reel with sink-tip line
- waterproof coat and hat
- sandwiches and thermos flask
- extra sweater
- plastic fish bags
- a folded bin bag to cover the game bag, and anything else to be stored, if it rains

It is a long time since I sat down in the river at night but, having said that, I shall probably do so the next time I go peal fishing! So it is wise to leave a bag in the car containing a spare set of clothes: socks, pants, shirt, trousers, sweater and a handkerchief. A towel is always useful. In fact, a small zipped bag holding these items is in my car throughout the fishing season.

Magnetic rod clips are my choice for carrying rods outside the car. One is placed on the front of the bonnet, and the other on the front of the roof. When the car is left unattended they can be lifted off and placed inside the vehicle. Rod clips which are tightened by a wing nut to the car gutter can be unscrewed and stolen.

Arrival at the River

Whether you fish alone or with a companion is a personal matter. If you are unsteady on your feet or nervous, it is sensible to have a companion, provided he does not fish too close to you and is not a chatterbox. Sea-trout fishing requires knife-edged concentration, which is impossible whilst talking. Personally, except when teaching I always fish alone and have never been badly frightened. Once when I heard grunting noises on the bank I waded ashore to find nothing more dangerous than a pair of mating hedgehogs.

On another occasion, whilst fishing in the small hours, I saw the headlights of a car come

Magnetic rod carriers for short journeys to the river with tackle made up ready for use. Do not exceed 50 mph!

down the road, stop and go out beside my own parked car. Thinking it might be a thief trying to break in to steal the radio, I crept across the field to see that the parked vehicle was a police car. The officer had his back to me and was peering into my car through the rear window. In rubber boots I approached silently from behind and said, over his shoulder, 'Can I help you, officer?' He went straight up into the air, turned around whilst airborne and, before descending with a thump managed to eject the words, 'What's your name, then?' Breathing heavily, his pulse racing, he explained that he was looking for sheep poachers.

There is no reason for fear. The countryside and the river are the same by night as during the day, but some creatures which are active at night do make disturbing noises. This is not frightening if you know what is making the noise. So to be relaxed while fishing at night one has to gather experience of the countryside and its wild inhabitants.

Time your journey so that you arrive at the river about 45 minutes before you anticipate it will be dark enough to start fishing. Go to the pool closest to the car, deposit your game bag, then walk to the most distant place you intend to fish. In this way you will do half of your walking in the light and, if you fish back towards your car, you will finish near it later in the night. A long walk to the car after three hours of fishing, possibly carrying several pounds of peal, demonstrates a lack of planning.

At the place you intend to start, unhook the fly, rub down the leader with sink-mix, and place the fly and leader to soak in the river. If they are left in the water until you are ready to start fishing, they will sink under the water at the first cast. Nylon skating on the river surface may deter a sea-trout from taking the fly.

Now sit on the bank to watch and wait for the light to go. Waiting is a test of patience, but there is much to see and hear. Ducks fly up the valley at dusk to glean fallen grain in the harvest

Whilst waiting for full darkness, wipe the leader with sink-mix, then leave it to soak in the river.

field; carrion crows fly silently, black and shadow-like, to roost against the ivy-covered trunks of trees, and a heron slides down from the sky on soft grey wings. I have often wondered whether herons are able to see to fish at night, and have come to the conclusion that they are. Certainly, they glide down to alight in the field a few yards from the bank and then stalk forward to the edge of the river. Why would they do this, other than to fish?

As dusk takes over from day, lights are switched on in the cottages nearby, and bats come out of hollow trees to hawk flies over the river. If you catch a bat on a fly whilst casting, you will notice that they are usually hooked in the wing. This is because they scoop flies out of the air in their wings, transfer them to the flap of skin between their legs and then flip them up into their mouths. The mouth of a bat is small and unsuited to catching flies at speed in the air. Swallows,

swifts and house and sand martins, on the other hand, have mouths almost as wide as their bodies, like trout they are thus able to gather food in the mouth whilst moving at considerable speed.

With the approach of dusk sea-trout start to leap. They go straight up 1 or 2 ft into the air like shining Polaris missiles, except that they then splash down to send waves across the pool. Wait another ten minutes, just to be on the safe side. You can start when it is hard to make out details on the far bank, and you can no longer distinguish colours.

If you find waiting intolerable, there is nothing wrong with fishing rough water in the half light – you may take a salmon by swimming a wet fly down a pool neck. A friend of mine is sometimes rewarded in the twilight by fishing a skidding waterproofed mayfly across the river, and another caught two 5-lb peal on a deer-hair sedge at dimity, the Devon word for dusk.

Where to Cast

When night arrives, take up your rod and move to the position from which you intend to start casting. This is not necessarily the stand from which you expect to achieve the best results, it is the position from which you can cover close water, avoiding disturbing nearby fish by wading.

Do not start by sending your fly speeding above the river to fall beneath the far bank. A long cast

CASTING IN A FAST FLOW

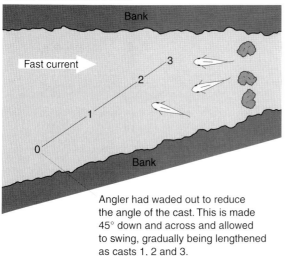

Angler had waded out to reduce the angle of the cast. This is made 45° down and across and allowed to swing, gradually being lengthened as casts 1, 2 and 3.

PUTTING A CURVE IN THE RETRIEVED PATH OF A FLY

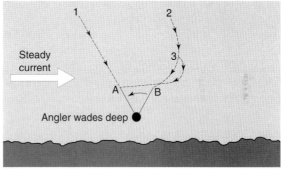

Rod in position A casts to 1, rod moves to B following fly round to 2, rod swings upstream to starting position A. This puts a pronounced curve in the passage of the speeded-up fly from 3, stimulating a fish to take. The principle is the same as a fly curving behind a drifting boat, and in a backed-up salmon fly.

CASTING IN A STEADILY FLOWING POOL

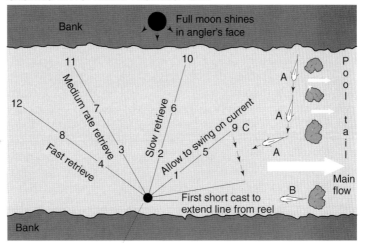

Angler in water below bank facing moon. No silhouette.

Head-up, tail-down tube starts to skate at C, attracts fish at B, and fish A which has followed and is stimulated to take as tube head surfaces.

is likely to 'line' and frighten peal which are over-reached and have no chance to see the fly. Instead, kneel if you are on the bank and make a short cast almost straight downstream, allow it to swing to the dangle position and then retrieve. Without extending the distance, make the next cast down and across at 30 degrees from the bank, allow it to swing and dangle, and retrieve. Then do the same at 45 degrees, straight out at 90 degrees, and make two or three throws upstream in a similar arc. The downstream throws should be allowed to swing in on the current with very little line retrieval; the upstream projections must be recovered at a rate faster than the water flow, or the fly will drift in a lifeless manner.

Having covered the water through an arc of almost 180 degrees at a radius of 4 or 5 yd, extend an additional yard of line and repeat the search. When an area of water up to a distance of about 10 yd has been covered you can stand up; this will help to keep longer back casts lifted above the bank to the rear whilst extending your forward distance to 15 yd.

You now have to decide whether to extend a longer line or wade towards the fish in the middle of the river and under the far bank. My preference is to wade and cast a distance of about 45 ft. A short cast can be placed with accuracy and delicacy; a long cast may splash down, disturbing the fish, and the fly will be covering an area not readily seen except in bright moonlight. Most of my fish are hooked within a radius of 60 ft, and many take at 40 ft. This is possible because I move like a wraith.

Once positioned with the water halfway up the thighs, little of the angler is visible to the fish, even those nearby. It is surprising how close unsuspecting sea-trout will approach if you do not move your feet, and do not send out warning waves of water. All movements, other than casting, should be slow and deliberate. Stand like a statue. New arrivals to the pool will not necessarily consider that an angler represents danger. I have often had salmon and sea-trout leap,

spraying me with water as they fall back into the river.

The upstream cast produces almost as many fish as the downstream one, and fish hooked above you are usually secure. This solid hooking is probably due to the fish having to take the fly at a faster speed than a lure cast downstream and swinging slowly across the current. Without doubt one experiences many more twitches at the fly as it searches the river downstream of the angler, and this must be due to the fish having more time to investigate.

I like an upstream throw with a rapid line recovery. Sea-trout cannot see directly to their rear, and thus one is likely to be casting from a blind area. If one is standing in the tail of a pool just before the river breaks into the next stickle, one is usually in shallow water; the area above is deeper. And although there are exceptions, heavy peal are most likely to lie in deep areas than shallow glides. So although an upstream cast produces fewer peal than a downstream one, the fish are often substantial. A further advantage of standing in the shallow tail is that one hooks fish in deep water above, but plays them in the shallower area where their companions are not disturbed. There is a risk that a hooked fish may dash past you into the fast rapids below, but this is rare.

To be able to fish from both sides of a river is an advantage; one may then cast from the shallow side to deeper water midstream and under the far bank. This allows one to enter the river from a gently shelving bank which probably provides a smoothly descending sand or gravel edge on which fish can be beached. The area where a hooked fish is to be played should be away from his companions in a shoal, for you will be trying for these when you resume casting.

In certain areas of the river you may be forced to fish from the deep side towards the shallow. This can be dangerous in that a step forward could plunge you into water of an uncomfortable depth. It also places you above some of the sea-trout you hope to catch. These fish will be scared

The tails of pools are 'hot spots' for night sea-trout fishing.

out of the area as soon as you start casting, and any peal hooked will be played and netted close to their companions if these have not already departed.

The majority of sea-trout are caught towards the tails of pools which are deep on one side and overhung on that side by trees and bushes. It also happens, less frequently, that peal are caught in the necks of pools. It must be remembered that sea-trout migrate up the river and therefore have to cover the whole length of a pool and work their way through stickles. They not only travel via deep channels, but sometimes flap through shallow water running between half-dry stones. Why they select the hard way is a mystery, but the evidence is there – flapping sounds at night.

Welcome these noises when you are fishing an area into which the flappers must swim; the necks of pools hold travelling fish for short periods. It is worth fishing the run-in, but do not spend too much time on these narrow, fast places. They are worth a cast or two whilst moving between pools, or more detailed attention in the half-light at dusk.

Some years ago I taught groups of four boys sea-trout fishing in the dark. They fished in pairs, each couple being provided with a CB radio with which to contact me in the dark. Once I had an incoherent but triumphant request for assistance. On arrival I found a 14-year-old boy with a 2½-lb peal taken from the deep narrow neck of the Manse. It was in his net, well mixed up in the

Moving with a wading staff. (*Tony Allen*)

Using the net handle as a wading probe. (*Tony Allen*)

Hooking the net on to the Hang-All Belt Loop requires both hands. (*Tony Allen*)

TYPICAL SEA-TROUT POOL

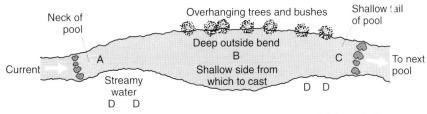

A – Streamy rippled water may be fished first in the half-light at dusk. Fish intending to run upstream from B, and from lower down the river, pass through in the dark and may be caught.

B – Slack deep water daytime resting area of sea-trout.

C – Main taking area. Resident fish move from B to C at dusk. First pausing place of fish arriving from lower down the river.

D – Cast from shallow side towards deep water. Do not stand on high opposite bank above deep water.

meshes with a pair of short handled coal tongs and his personally-dressed treble-hooked tube fly. Not having a priest, he had thrust the tongs into his belt when he left home!

How Long to Fish a Lie

If one is fishing a lake stocked with trout, and there are other anglers nearby, it is noticeable that several may catch a trout almost at the same time, after hours of fishless casting. It is often the same with sea-trout.

There is no doubt that, from June to September, on clement nights, the first two hours of darkness are generally the most productive, although not always – one cannot lay down rules. One may often fish for an hour or more without a touch, and then be rewarded. One night, I fished with two companions from 8.45 pm until 11.30 pm in early September. Six fish were taken, with one of 3½ lb. Two nights later we fished the same hours without a touch, in what seemed to be similar conditions. Determined, we continued and between 11.30 pm and 1.30 am we took nine peal and three brown trout.

A friend of mine fished the tail of the Manse one night.

> 15th July 1989. One peal 2 lb 12 oz. A No 8 White Lure with red tag. Fished the first hour with a Black Lure then, at 12.05 took the peal casting upstream with the white fly.

For some reason, the fish must suddenly have come on the take.

Personally, as I have said I like to go to the farthest pool and fish there for as long as peal are coming to the net or plucking and pulling. If there is no response after an hour I move upstream to the next pool. I have often fished for one or two hours without any encouragement and then taken a substantial peal. In fact it seems that nights when there is little activity produce peal of high average weight after midnight. One cannot be dogmatic, but it is worth remembering that

peal move about and new occupants arrive, and one of these new arrivals, in its initial swim-around inspection of the area, may take your passing fly.

The river may appear lifeless in the middle of the night; activity slows and frequent jumping ceases, with just an occasional splash. Fish have 'gone down'. The experience is similar to the cessation of a hatch of olives on a chalk stream – trout stop rising. Some anglers, myself included, stop at this stage and go home. Others take up a rod with a sinking line, but this does not work for me as the fly catches on the bedrock in our shallow, slow-moving pools. I sometimes fish on in summer to see the dawn; activity increases for a short spell as the midsummer sky lightens in the north-east.

Hooking, Playing and Landing

Imagine that you are standing with me halfway down my Embankment Pool. We have waded out from the shallow right bank until the water is above our knees. The riverbed is smooth and sandy and we both feel secure. One can start from a wading position in this pool, as the area to be searched by the fly is wide and peal lie in the centre, on the far side, and right in the tail near the right bank. There are no fish on this side other than in the 2–3-yd glide ahead of the line where the water breaks into the rough area of the run-off. That place is some yards away and will be covered as we progress down the pool.

I know this because I have fished the pool so many times. This is one reason for thoroughly learning a beat on a river. Go to the same pools, season after season – the experience you gain will be rewarded with satisfactory catches which would elude the stranger. Do not go in search of the river where the rainbow ends. Learn one section of one river until you have a detailed knowledge of the lies, and of the moods of that water.

There is a tree on my right, on the right bank,

Fish with the rod point low to register the slightest touch to the fly . . .

. . . and with the line at an angle to cushion shock takes.

When using a fly with a flying treble hook the points may catch in the net meshes. With small peal, up to 2 lb, take them out by hand.

so I cast right-handed over my left shoulder whilst you stand to my right out of the area of the passage of the airborne fly. Out goes the fly downstream at about 30 degrees from our bank; the ring in the water where it alights is clearly visible. The white line is also easy to see as it swings, pushed by the current into a slight curve, to hang below us. Nothing. I know a fish has not touched the fly because the rod tip during this line swing has been 2–3 in above the water surface, the rod has pointed along the floating line to the fly and the fingers of my left hand have been on the line just ahead of the reel and behind the forefinger of my right hand. If a fish had touched the fly the

slightest tweak would have been transmitted through leader and line to my left fingers. The forefinger of my right hand, which is holding the rod, is extended in a crook, over which the line passes. If I retrieve the line by two or three pulls of 1 yd each to increase the speed of passage across the river, the crook grip against the cork butt is relaxed as I draw line in with my left hand. As my left hand moves forward to take another grip before making a further recovery, I tighten the crooked forefinger of my right hand. Thus the line is always secured by one hand or the other against a sudden pull when a fish takes the fly.

Whilst I am still standing in the same place, I draw another yard of line from the reel to extend the arc covered by the fly. I repeat this process until the lure is falling at a distance of 12–15 yd. There is no response. I shuffle forward two or three steps. No waves, no stumbles. A glance to my right establishes that we are now level with a gorse bush on our bank. Any moment now! When I reach the gorse bush and make an easy cast, not stretching for distance, I am covering the peal – if they are there tonight. There is a little ledge of rock on the riverbed in that place, and peal lie before the ridge in comfort, with the flow passing overhead. The line twitches – nothing more. A peal, a small schoolie probably. That lie is not chosen by senior fish. If there is one schoolie, there are probably several. We continue casting to that spot until we catch a fish or tweaking ceases. Cast, swing, retrieve; cast, swing, retrieve. Then, – *splash* – the rod jerks up automatically, arcs over and the line lifts and points to the white flurry. Without doubt a little peal. Heavy fish tend to boil and surge on being hooked; schoolies splash. The rod should now be raised almost to the vertical to act as a shock-absorbing spring. The fish moves rapidly upstream. I recover line as she passes me, by stripping in over the forefinger. Then, lacking weight, she steadies 10 yd away across the river. Now is the pause in which to reel in the stripped line floating downstream on the river in a long loop.

If a fish is netted whilst you are wading, knock it on the head over the net, then slip it into the fish bag . . .

. . . or wade ashore.

If it is not recovered onto the reel it may become entangled in the fish and the leader when the landing or netting moment arrives.

The fish is now drawn close and we have to decide whether to net, beach or pick out by hand. Beaching would mean wading ashore. Netting risks the hook catching in the net meshes, particularly if the lure is the flying treble Night Prowler. So we use the hand for a small fish. Whether by hand or net, the right moment arrives when the fish is beaten and turns on its side. One can always see the light-coloured upturned flank. Always wait to see that still silver/grey patch. Do not scoop about with the net in the dark water for

an invisible fish. With a small fish of about 1 lb I reach forward with my left hand, grip the fish with my thumb and forefinger pressing in the gills and the palm of my hand over his back. I shove the rod butt into the top of my left thigh boot with my right hand, take out the priest and dispatch the fish with a couple of thumps on the back of the head. I then remove the hook and slide the fish into the bag hanging on my belt loop. Neither torch has been used.

If the peal is too small to be kept, I still take it out by hand, having first dipped my hand in the river to prevent the fish being burned by a hot palm. The grip should now be along the whole

Above and right: Uses of the flat torch.

body, taking care not to damage the gills. If a light is needed to remove the hook, turn your back on the area being fished, and use the red filter torch, which does not have to be held as it is clipped, pointing outwards, to the belt.

We continue down the pool until we reach the place from which we can cover the 2–3 yd of smooth glide above the run-off. Here lie heavier specimens, which rarely pluck and twitch. They take with a surge of power, run 4 or 5 yd and leap. I drop my rod point when a peal leaps, and tighten when it has fallen back into the river, but some anglers do not slacken on an airborne fish. My reason for doing so can be demonstrated as follows. Swing your arm in the air, then swing it under water, and notice the difference. The former movement is violent and fast; the second is damped down by water resistance. In the same way rapid airborne movement by a fish is danger-ous, as the hook hold comes under severe stress. If you drop the rod point whilst the fish is in the air there is no pull on the hook, which is held in place by the barb.

Changing the fly by the use of the swan-necked torch.

A heavy peal may pull off 20 yd of line in an immediate upstream rush and jump. During the run, keep the rod point high to hold as much line out of the water as possible, even to the extent of raising your arms above your head. Drowned line drags on the hook and increases the chance of loss when a heavy fish jumps some distance away. After this rush the fish may streak downstream towards you; there is no time to reel, so strip. He will then settle, boring deep at a distance of 5 or 6 yd. Take advantage of the pause to recover the stripped line onto the reel. The final phase, wallowing, comes as a surprise. The fish, which may have been either in the air or under the surface, comes into view. You may have thought he was several yards to your right or left, but there he is, a rod's length away. Unclip the net, flick it open and trap it between your left upper rod arm and your body. Move the fish closer, extend the net in your right hand when his side is flat on the surface, sink the metal ring, draw him over and lift. Confusion now ensues!

Move by move, proceed as follows. Hold the net steady with one hand on the shaft/ring hinge, push the rod butt into storage down the inside of your left wader, withdraw the priest, place the net handle under your left armpit and take hold of the fish with your left hand *over the net*. Now, knock him on the head, remove the hook and slide the fish into the fish bag. All this can, and should, be done while still wading if you are in an area from which you do not wish to move. In fact, if the fish is in the 3–4-lb category I am usually so delighted that I wade ashore with the fish in the net and dispatch him there, before indulging in long moments of admiration and self-congratulation, followed by some sadness that so beautiful a creature has been brought to an end.

After landing a heavy peal the fly should be re-tied. Carefully check the strength of the leader at Turle and tucked half blood knots on single- or treble-hooked flies, for a prolonged battle weakens nylon at the knot.

The simplest way to secure a fish is to beach it on a gently shelving edge to the river. This can only be done if you are fishing from the side in such a place or are prepared to wade to the bank. Later in this chapter Brian Easterbrook describes how he was forced to beach a 10½-lb peal in the dark because his net was too small. To beach a fish, first play it out. Then, by rod pressure, draw it towards the sand or mud sloping into the water, or a stone slab at river level. With the rod horizontal over the ground keep up the pressure until the head of the fish is aground. Now circle to the rear and push it up the bank.

Be careful of bats. I welcome them because they are a sign of prolific insect life on warm nights. Peal also like soft air, so my chances are good. But bats are nuisances because they pluck at moving fly lines being retrieved on the water surface. At first I did not believe that a bat could flick at my fly line, but they are attracted to moving objects and locate the line by their echo-sounding radar systems. As you feel your floating line with your fingers as the fly moves through the water, remember that solid plucks are peal, twitches are bats.

Using One's Senses

At night I fish with my mouth open, as it is a silent way of breathing. All my senses are tuned to reception. The pupils of my eyes are wide and my ears receive the slightest sound within their range. My cheeks feel the direction of the wind, and my hands gauge the temperatures of the air and the water. So far as is possible after centuries of soft living, the senses of my primeval ancestors are at full stretch.

Being in touch with the natural world and the moods of fish, water and weather enables the angler to place his fly in the right place at the right moment. When I wade out from the bank I am enveloped by the night. Darkness enfolds both me and the peal. I suspect they know I am there but, being some yards off, and being unlike their known predators, they are not alarmed. To connect me with the fly would be beyond their faculties. And so, quietly, one by one, I am able to pick them off.

I have watched many people who are just beginning to develop their sea-trout fishing ability. Their problems are not lack of information on the lies of fish, incorrect flies or unsuitable tackle. They know about these matters. Their problems are clumsiness and failing to blend into the world of the sea-trout and the river. Fishing in the dark without being noticed by fish is an ability which may be acquired by the steady development of the physical senses, not least of which is feeling forward with one's feet along the riverbed.

Fishing the Wake Lure

When I was writing one of my earlier books, *The River Test* the then Head Keeper to the Houghton Club, Mick Lunn, granted me an interview. Talking of fly-fishing ethics he said of nymph fishing:

> They may start [casting] upstream, then it is a bit square and then, before you know where you are, the nymph is trickling about below. That is not playing the game. *Neither is the dragging mayfly.*

Upstream casting with dry fly or nymph is the rule on the chalk rivers. If you ask, 'Why not a dragging mayfly?', my reply is, 'Because it is not imitative, but particularly, because it is too successful'.

A sea-trout is a migratory brown trout. If river trout rush after, and grab, a dragging mayfly, where is the mystery in peal following suit? There is no mystery – they do. A wake-creating mayfly as it skims across the river downstream of the angler leaves a 'V' track on the surface, but it is soon stopped by an open mouth – not always, but sometimes and in some places more than others. Just like anything else to do with sea-trout, on some nights the system works, and on others the wake lure is ignored.

The operation is straightforward. A light-coloured floating fly line and a knotless tapered OX leader connect one to a well-waterproofed fly. The leader should be greased along the 6 ft closest to the fly line, and the final yard of nylon terminating at the fly left ungreased. The flies are described in Chapter 2, their features are bulk and floatability.

All pools are not suited to the wake lure; the best water is where there is a glide of medium speed and smooth surface. The lure is cast down and across. Just as the current sweeps a subsurface lure across the river under the water skin, it does the same to a wake lure on the surface. If one moves steadily down a pool, the first thing a stationary peal will see is the fly as it swings across the surface of his window. The line will be upstream and out of his circle of vision. He may follow the lure, taking as it swings or, the line having straightened below the angler, as the fly is retrieved. The curving path of a fly as it straightens behind a boat on a loch, or is swept around by the wind when an angler fishes a stillwater from the bank, is always more attractive than a straight passage.

The essentials in wake-lure fishing are that the lure floats and that it does not stop dragging and thus producing a 'V' trail. The speed of movement across the river is controlled by the current and whether the angler retrieves line – the slower the water speed the faster one has to recover line. The path of the lure should not terminate in a shallow area downstream of the angler; peal do not like to follow into water where there is not the security of reasonable depth. Find a place where the lure will drag across a glide to hang momentarily, still creating a wake, over deep water downstream of the rod.

Wake-lure fishing is exciting, more so than fishing the subsurface lure, because one sees fish take the fly. It has been said that the darkest nights are best for this style of fishing, but it depends on one's interpretation of the word 'best'. If it is construed as meaning that catches are heavier than on moonlit nights, that is probably true. But if excitement is the object, even though catches may be moderate, a moonlit night tops the poll. In earlier years I failed to interpret what I saw by moonlight – a slight movement behind the dragging fly. There is little doubt that a tiny rupture of the gliding river surface a yard behind the fly is caused by the dorsal fin of a stalking peal. Three times this happened to me on one night. I cannot be certain that I am right, for the movement on that cast did not terminate in a take, but the next swing of the fly produced a fish. What else would break the surface?

The Dropper

I rarely fish a dropper. Some skilled anglers catch peal on a bob fly, and others even fish three flies, adding a dropper between the point and bob flies.

But the more flies one has, the greater the chance of a tangle if one is landing fish with a net, as the hooks pierce the strands of the meshes. This problem does not arise if the fish can be beached, provided one does not have to wade ashore to do it and thus disturb the pool. In my view it is most unwise to use more than two flies, and even then tangles may arise when casting unless there is a pronounced elipse in the line when false casting overhead.

The bob fly should be attached to the main leader by a short length of 10-lb Maxima – 4 in is sufficient. If the dropper or bob fly nylon is too long it will become wrapped about the main leader. To attach a bob fly, take a short length of 10-lb nylon and tie it against the 20-lb Maxima

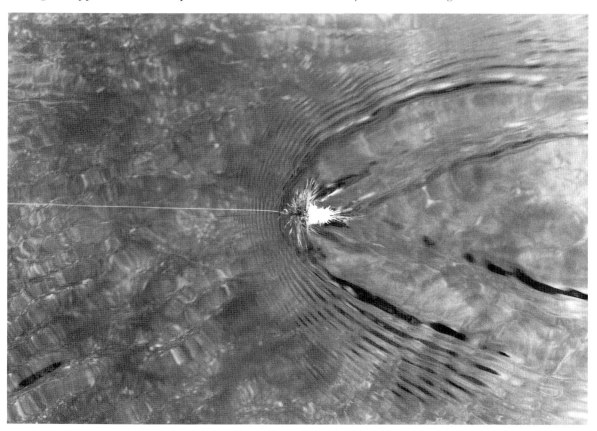

The 'V' wake of a surface lure.

with a tucked half blood knot just above the blood knot of the 20 lb/15 lb junction of your home-made leader. Then slide the tucked half blood down to rest against the blood knot. You can use a tucked half blood to attach the bob fly to this short length of nylon, because there is not enough length to use the two-turn Turle. It is also possible to tie on a bob fly by leaving one end of a blood knot long. The end is the continuation of the top leader section, so that if the knot comes undone the fish is still attached. A water knot can also be used. The disadvantage of these two methods is that the 20-lb Maxima is too thick for the fly to work properly.

Now the fly. A No 8 Black Muddler is as good as any other pattern in creating a wake in this position. It should be lighter than the point fly, which is the case if you use 1-in tubes like the Silver Stoat's Tail or Alexandra tube. This is an important point; the point fly must be heavier in order to extend the leader as the cast alights on the water.

A long rod of 9 ft 6 in or 10 ft helps one to scuttle the bob fly over the surface of the water, just as one might do when fishing from a boat in a loch or wading in a trout reservoir. A short rod cannot lift the bob fly to the surface until it is too close to the angler to have a lengthy skim across the top of the water.

A bob fly should be skittering over water of sufficient depth for the peal to follow. It is thus necessary to wade, or else to crouch below the bank on the deep side of a pool. Cast out at 90 degrees, let the flies swing around until they are at about 45 degrees, then raise the rod tip to lift the bob until it breaks through the surface and creates its 'V'. It is not necessary to grease the Muddler, which is only going to scuttle when the rod is raised. At the extremity of the cast, and in the early yards of the swing and retrieve, it will be fishing subsurface. The bob fly outfit can also be cast upstream on a short line and recovered with the rod held high; the line recovery should be faster than with the across and down-and-across casts.

Do not forget that you will have more tangles than with a single fly, so it is wise to have a replacement leader ready in a packet in your pocket. And remember that two or more flies are not for the beginner.

The Head-up-Tail-down Tube Fly

When fishing single-hooked subsurface lures, treble-hooked tubes and other lures such as the Night Prowler and the Burglar, I aim to keep them, and the leader, beneath the water surface. To this end I wipe sink-mix over the leader, and I avoid thick, heavily dressed lightweight shop-bought flies because it is impossible to make them sink. And I take considerable care to ensure that everything remains a couple of inches beneath the water surface when I am using a floating fly line.

One day I was teaching two or three pupils to fish our water so that they could return and give a good account of themselves that night. Wading into the pool and casting down and across, I gave a running commentary as the tube fly and leader swung across submerged, as I intended. Then, as the tube swung towards the run-off at the tail of the pool below me, where the current rises to flow over the shallow ridge of stones at the tail, the pupils shouted, 'Your fly is skating, Charles.' They were right. In the final 2 yd of swing, as the line straightened, the head of the tube poked above the surface to create a wake, whilst the treble hook remained submerged. One of them took my place whilst I watched the sequence. When cast upstream, across, or down and across, the fly stayed below the surface, but when it was almost fished out downstream its head poked up. It was aquaplaning, as it was fat along the silver-tinselled, slippery body.

This would not do at all. I applied sink-mix. A slow-sinking, 4-ft braided leader butt was suggested, or 2 ft of looped sink-tip line, to keep the outfit down. I tried the sink-tip, but it seemed unbalanced, splashing on the water when it was cast.

ABOVE. Dartmoor sea-trout and salmon spawning stream. Netting off a 65 yd section for juvenile electro-survey.

LEFT. Classifying the juvenile fishlets before they are returned to the stream.

BELOW. Night fly-fishing equipment.

Brian Easterbrook's 10½-lb peal.

River Dart. Large sea-trout are sometimes taken whilst salmon fishing by day.

The author dapping on the River Dart.

A folding seat placed across a boat raises the height of an angler.

ABOVE. River Taw. REFFIS instructor Roddy Rae roll-casting above King Bridge.

BELOW. River Taw. Small peal are sometimes found in rough water by day.

ABOVE. Rivers Taw and Mole. Hugh Dalgety fishes his Junction Pool as the light goes down.

BELOW. River Teign. The top of Drogo Pool, looking upstream.

ABOVE. River Teign. The sea-trout and salmon ladder at the tail of Drogo Pool

BELOW. River Dovey. Worming water under the trees.

ABOVE. River Dovey. Fly water off the shingle in a pool tail

BELOW. River Towy, the most productive sea-trout river in England and Wales. Part of the Golden Grove and Abercothi Fisheries.

River Towy. Max James, retired Head River Keeper, inspects the river at Llysthandy.

River Fowey. Ralph Hands casts his Horror fly with a spinning rod under Station Drive Bridge on the Lanhydrock Estate water of the National Trust.

ABOVE. River Fowey. There is little room to fish the fly on this river.
BELOW. Hampshire Avon. The Royalty Fishery. The Garden Pool

Hampshire Avon. The Royalty Fishery. The bridge at the top of Bridge Pool

Otter prints beside the river

ABOVE. River Lyd. Roy Buckingham fishes the tail of Jock Scott Pool.

BELOW. Rivers Tamar and Lyd. The cockpit tackle room at the Arundel Arms Hotel, Lifton.

ABOVE. The Border Esk. View of the river above Bentpath

BELOW. Border Esk. In this pool REFFIS instructor Tony King finds sea-trout under the first ash tree on the right bank . . .

. . . . and dresses a fly to catch them.

River Spey. Col (Retd) Tom Hawkins MBE points to a sea-trout lie below Old Spey Bridge.

ABOVE. River Dulnain, a tributary of the Spey. The river at Carrbridge.

BELOW. River Dulnain. REFFIS Guide David Herbert fishes a sea-trout pool

ABOVE. River Spey. Sea-trout lie under the trees on the left bank at Kincardine.
BELOW. River Strathmore, which feeds Loch Hope.

ABOVE. Loch Hope. Boats setting out on the South End of the Altnaharra Hotel water

BELOW. Loch Hope. The Keeper's House at the North End where he has charge of four boats and one on Middle Bay.

The track of the head-up-tail-down tube fly.

Whilst I was searching for a solution it penetrated the recesses of my mind that where the fly popped up was where, at night, I had caught many peal. If the fly head did not create a wake for the final 2 yd, those fish might not be caught. So leaving well alone, we continued as before, and sure enough fish hooked themselves in that place.

Perhaps the explanation for this lies in a comparison with fishing a team of three flies from a boat for trout and sea-trout in a loch. Using a long rod, the team is cast out and retrieved, and when it is close to the boat the bob and then the dropper 'escape' into the air after a short trickle across the surface. My tube, at night in the lifting current at the pool run-off, was in the first stage of head-up escape and therefore had to be grabbed by the fish before it could get away.

The Sink-tip Pool

I said in Chapter 2 that the greater part of my fishing is with a floating fly line. No doubt this is also the case with many anglers, as a light-coloured floater is visible on the water, easily controlled and more pleasant to fish than a sinking line. It is also suited to my water, where the best sea-trout areas are not deep. Nevertheless, the sinking line has a place late at night in areas where the fly will not snag on the riverbed. A fly will not catch on bedrock if the pool is deep and the current, or the rate of retrieve, is fast enough to hold it clear. So a slow-sinking line or sink-tip may be suitable in waters of medium depth; the type of line, fast or slow sinking, should match the pool.

When fishing a lake or reservoir for trout there are occasions, particularly in cold water, but also in a heat-wave, when a sinking fly line is one way to take the fly down to the fish and catch them. It is the same with sea-trout. One must not fish in just one way, waiting for the specific conditions that match that method. In fact, many people do not even wait for the conditions to suit the method; they fish their style all the time, but only catch fish when their standard outfit and style suit the weather and the water. It is important to vary one's lines, flies and place of fishing to match the state of the river and the weather.

The chances of a catch with a fly on or just above the riverbed were brought home to me some years ago. I was fishing in a deep part of the Manse, using a floating line and a Teal & Silver of about No 8 size. There are large sea-trout in that place, which are visible when they leap at night and through polarized spectacles by day. During my daylight inspections I creep up on the place to peer through the leaves of an elder bush and the green stalks and white flowers of cow parsley. The pool is usually occupied by substantial fish weighing 2 or 3 lbs. Resting just above the bed they open their mouths from time to time, showing the white edges of their jaws. But put a fly over them by day and they just melt away.

I stood there one night, knee deep, casting with a floating line. The moon was up and to my right. A little stream enters the river at that place – as was apparent when it trickled off the high bank into the top of my right boot! Resting the rod on the bank, with the line, leader and fly extended over the river at the full extent of a cast, I emptied the boot. Picking up the rod I found myself connected to an athletic peal of about 5 lb. I think it was a peal, but there are also grilse in that place. The Olympic high jump would have been no problem to that fish, nor the 25-metre sprint, if

there is one. He would have taken a gold medal in both and was never seen again after those fearful leaps. My reward was a discovery – fish deep when standing beside the trickling stream.

When I was fly-fishing for salmon on the River Test at Broadlands in the 1970s, when the estate catch was in the region of 250–300 fish, I used a floating fly line and sometimes had difficulty in stopping the fly from skating. Bernard Aldrich, the Head Keeper, advocated a floating line with a short sinking tip. This arrangement fishes the fly just beneath the surface and can also be used for sea-trout fishing; a 4-ft sinking braided leader on the tip of the fly line would produce the same result. Braided leaders had not been invented in those days.

In what I call a 'sink-tip pool' one needs to present the fly at a lower level than one can achieve with a sinking braided leader or short sink-tip. The full 11-ft sinking section of an AirCel Supreme sink-tip line carries the fly down to the right depth if the line is retrieved slowly. The floating part of this line is light green. When fishing in moonlight, or on a bright night, it is possible to see when only about 1 ft of the light coloured floating line is outside the rod tip at the end of a retrieve. At this point the sinking tip can easily be lifted out of the river into the back cast. The length of line extended beneath the surface towards the end of a retrieve is much more difficult to judge with a fully sinking line.

There is another deep area on my beat which can only be reached satisfactorily in body waders, so I give it a miss because I prefer thigh boots. But I mean to try that lie this summer with a sink-tip. My interest has been aroused by my observations and by one particular incident. I have noticed that heavy peal leap there during the day and in the evening. It could be that they move elsewhere at night; perhaps some do, but I know that they do not all shift to shallower areas in the tail of the pool, because I hooked one in the leaping lie. It was at 1.30 am, which is late for me, and I was fishing a floating weight-forward line, 9-lb point and a No 8 Teal & Blue, when the fly just reached the spot at the end of a long throw. I was sleepy, I had lost concentration and depression had set in, for not a fish had been helpful. The rod tip was down at water level. Suddenly there was a tremendous jerk and 10 yd of line were stripped out. Before I had time to wake up and raise the rod tip to act a a spring, the fish swirled and the nylon snapped at the Turle knot. So that place must receive attention in body waders with a sink-tip line this coming season.

Avoiding Disasters

The aim of this book is to encourage you, not deter you, but there are certain problems which may arise if you are not careful. Confidence comes through catching fish, and if you can avoid problems *before* they arise, you will increase your catches and your confidence.

Replace your hooks as soon as it becomes necessary. Inspect them regularly whilst fishing. Feel the point in the dark; drag it across the flat of a finger nail to see how sharp it is. Are all three points of a treble fine-pointed, or has one been blunted by hitting a rock on the forward or back casts, or been damaged on the bedrock? Has the point of a single been bent towards the shank? Be sure to replace a hook after landing a heavy fish which may have slightly opened the bend.

Inspect your net. An old net may be rotten. A new one may have a hole in the meshes where it has been torn by a bramble or barbed wire. Check bags regularly and have a replacement available in the tackle cupboard at home. If the bag does not sink when it is extended beneath a fish being drawn over the net mouth, complications may arise. Ensure that the net bag sinks by clipping a sliver of copper or lead to the bottom meshes.

Do not try to net a sea-trout too soon. Always wait until it is played out on the surface. The moment the light-coloured flank shows flat on the river, that is the time to extend the net and draw the fish over the white-painted rim. Try not to allow a tired fish to move downstream in a strong current so that you have to pull it upstream to the net.

Do not allow loose line to trail in the river. When playing a sea-trout one often has to strip in line to maintain contact. Recover this onto the reel as soon as possible, particularly before you come to net a fish. You can tread on loose line when you are fishing from the beach and it will float downstream when you are wading. Floating line may become entangled in the fish if he swims into a position downstream.

Do not allow loose coils of line to develop on the reel. When recovering line onto a reel, spread from side to side of the spool with a guiding finger on the rod as you wind. If you do not do this, line will build up in large coils on one side and collapse over smaller-diameter coils on the other side of the spool. This leads to loose coils, the line may not run out smoothly and a fish may be pulled up short while you are playing it and break the hook hold. Never unwind a reel to give line to a fish, as this is a sure way of loosening the line on a reel.

Beware of grit in the reel. This may cause fish to be lost through stoppage. With most reels the spool can be removed and washed in the river. No harm is done by washing both the spool and the housing to remove grit. It is not necessary to wade out of the water in order to do this cleaning; press the rod down a thigh boot so that your hands are free.

The best course is not to allow grit to enter the reel in the first place. Do not place a wet reel, or any reel for that matter, on dry or wet sand – the grains will stick to the metal. In a heavy rainstorm do not place a reel on a stone at a low level if it is surrounded by sand; the grains will splash up onto the reel. Rest it on grass.

Clean and oil your reels. Many trout anglers have had their reels for a number of seasons and then come to learn sea-trout fishing with the same equipment. Some may not have seen an oil can for years and may be stiff in the action. On others the backing may be joined to the fly line by a whipping; if so, be sure the silk is sound.

Replace needle-knots regularly. You may recall that one of the methods I suggested for joining the fly line to the leader is to needle-knot 1 ft of 20-lb Maxima nylon into the end of the fly line. Of course, this will gradually shorten as leaders are changed and it must then be replaced, and a new needle-knot tied. If only the 10- 15-lb sections of the leader are renewed, after several weeks of fishing the needle-knot may weaken through constant flexing. Be sure the fly line does not lose strength where it enters the knot. Cut off the line just above the knot and replace the 1-ft length of 20-lb nylon, thus renewing the needle-knot. Tapered fly lines usually have a 2-ft level tip to allow such shortening from time to time without affecting the taper.

Slugs and **mink** can cause problems. Do not leave your fish uncovered on the bank whilst you fish elsewhere or wade in the river. Slugs enjoy a fish meal, and it is not pleasant to pick up your catch from the grass and find a slimy slug in the palm of your hand. Place the fish in a plastic bag, preferably white and thus easily located. My local grocer has good-quality white polythene carrier bags, and I store these throughout the year for summer use. It is also a good idea to hang the bag in a tree. I once had a 5-lb grilse pulled away many yards into thick cover by a mink. If you take a dog with you, the mink will stay away, and you will also have company.

Do not play fish too hard. When playing a salmon you can make him jump by applying too much rod pressure; the same goes for sea-trout. There is some risk of losing a leaping peal; slacken the pressure and he will settle to fight in the river, not in the air.

Check regularly for wind knots. These reduce the breaking strain of nylon by 50 per cent so make frequent checks. Do not try to undo them; carry spare spools of 10- 15-lb nylon for the point and middle sections, and replace these lengths.

Do not fish fine nylon. You have a duty to the sea-trout not to allow them to get away with a fly in the mouth and 3 ft of trailing 4-lb monofilament. There is always the chance of breakage, of course, but you can reduce the risks if the leader point at night is not less than 8 lb in strength. Another precaution is to re-tie the fly after landing a heavy fish, as the nylon will probably have weakened at the knot attaching the fly.

Stick to one fly, especially when you are first starting. Beginners should avoid droppers. A fish or two may be caught on a bob fly, but a lot of time will be lost undoing tangles. Progress to two flies if you want to, but only when you are thoroughly capable of handling your tackle in the dark.

Brian Easterbrook's 10½-lb Peal

23 September 1992. 8.00 pm. 10½-lb hen. Length 2ft 7 in. Girth 1 ft 4 in. River Dart.

When he caught this fish, Brian was using a 9-ft carbon rod with a DT6F light-coloured fly line, so that the colour gave an indication of the position of the fly in the dark. The leader was home-made in sections of monofilament joined by blood knots: top section 23 lb, middle section 15 lb, point 10 lb. The 23-lb top section was joined to the fly line by a nail knot.

His fly was an Alexandra on a 1 in-unweighted plastic tube with a No 10 treble.

Body: Flat silver tinsel, ribbed silver wire
Wing: 14 pieces of peacock sword tail, seven on each side
Cheeks: Jungle cock
Silk: Black Naples.

This is his account of what happened.

> I started to fish just after dark, making three or four casts just outside a small stone I know close to my bank. I then cast further out, felt a knock and struck into a fish. The battle began. The fish, when hooked, leapt about 5 ft into the air, and another angler, fishing nearby, thought I had

fallen in! There were five or six jumps all over the pool. I got him in close, but he wasn't having any and shot up to the top of the pool – then down to the bottom. I thought he would go out of the pool, but managed to turn him with powerful side strain. He then settled down, moving about the pool without jumping. I got him in close. The other angler came to help. We had to look at the fish to see the size. A torch revealed his vastness and the fact that he would not go into our nets. He had to be beached on the sand. Drawing him in he churned up a lot of mud and thus lost direction as he could not see. I grabbed him by the tail, which was as thick as a salmon, and carried him ashore to be attended to by the priest.

The night was warm and muggy, and a drizzle had just started. There was no moon and it was quite dark. The water level was medium/low.

Brian then froze the fish. It was set up and cased in 1994, and he sent me the flank scales I had requested. I sent them to Kelvin Broad at the National Rivers Authority, Exeter. This is his report.

Three of the four scales were 'regenerated' but luckily the fourth was clearly readable. This fish smolted at the age of three, then spent one winter at sea before returning to spawn in each of the following four years. It had returned to fresh water for the fifth time before capture in late September 1992. Hence the fish had a total age of eight years, having hatched in 1984.

The scene of the capture of Brian Easterbrook's 10½-lb peal.

CHAPTER 4

Spinning and Worming Tackle

If one is spinning for sea-trout with light tackle one must take into account the chance that a salmon may take the bait; and when one is after salmon, sea-trout may be enticed. The two fish overlap in size and also in their open seasons. When I have been spinning in summer for sea-trout in a spate, I have grassed two sea-winter salmon as well as grilse, and when I have been spinning for salmon in late March and April I have landed large sea-trout. Some peal on their third spawning runs exceed the average grilse in weight.

One should always try to avoid losing fish through monofilament lines and traces breaking, or a hook bending out. When I am after sea-trout, my equipment is capable of landing salmon but it is, on the whole, lighter and the nylon less strong than in a spring, heavy-water outfit. This has something to do with the size of fish, but it is mainly because I am normally fishing smaller, lighter-weight baits in shallower, warmer water when I am after sea-trout in summer.

Fly-fishing at night is more pleasurable in most water conditions than spinning, and the fly also accounts for more fish. Nevertheless, spun bait has a place in a spate when the fly is unsuitable and unproductive, and in low water when it is cast upstream by day.

Spinning Rods

The angler who fishes for salmon solely on small and medium rivers and does not want to fish the natural baits of worm, shrimp and prawn with a long rod is likely to rely on an 8 ft 6 in or 9-ft spinning rod. This must be capable of throwing 1 oz (28 g) of lure and additional weight. Such a rod has more power than is needed for small peal but, we may have the good fortune to meet a 10-lb salmon. As my salmon spinning takes place mainly on small and medium rivers I use an 8 ft 6 in Hardy Fibalite rod, and continue to spin for peal with this in summer – one rod for both fish.

If you are fishing for salmon on wide rivers choose a 10-ft rod capable of throwing 1½ oz (42 g) during spring and autumn outings in heavy water. If you are based on such a water, you will need an extra rod for sea-trout. The casting capacity need not be more than $^{11}/_{16}$ oz. (20 g). A long rod enables you to fish under the far bank without the bait being pulled downstream and rapidly across by a long belly of submerged monofilament.

The problem with some spinning rods is the excessive length of the butt, which is awkward when passing the rod across one's body from hand to hand during casting as the rubber bung on the end catches on one's clothes. I am not fat and my arms are not short, but one needs the arms of a gibbon to deal with the 30-in butts of some rods.

Before buying a rod make sure the reel mount is not too far up the butt or the pleasure of casting will be spoilt. Also inspect the butt ring above the reel mount. This should be at least ¼ in in diameter. If it is too small, line coming off a fixed spool reel in coils may bunch up at this point and limit your casting distance.

Carbon and fibreglass rods need little maintenance. In both cases rub the male spigot, where the two sections join, with candle wax from time to time. This protects the ends from wear, and helps to prevent the sections working loose during the day whilst casting. Inspect the tip ring for wear during the season. Lines pick up grit and other abrasive substances during use, and grooves are sometimes cut in this ring as the monofilament is cast out and reeled back. These ridges in the metal will damage the line. As with all rods, the line guide wrappings should be inspected during the close season and varnished if necessary. Rods should not be put in their sleeves when wet, and when in the sleeve they should be hung vertically without the sleeve ties being drawn tight.

Spinning Reels, Lines and Traces

Apart from old centre-pin reels, there are now two available designs: the multiplier and the fixed spool. The multiplier is not suited to light summer spinning; it has its place in early- and late-season salmon fishing in heavy water with substantial baits. This is because one needs sufficient weight in the terminal tackle when casting, to overcome the inertia of the reel drum and keep it revolving. Moreover, plenty of room is needed to build up momentum in the bait and weight; this requires a

A fixed-spool spinning reel is suited to flicking out a spinning bait or worm in restricted circumstances.

full swing of the rod, which is likely to be impossible in thickly bushed and overgrown areas.

We do not usually sally forth to spin solely for sea-trout in cold full spring rivers; we normally go after this fish in warmer conditions in summer, with lightweight baits in rivers which are mainly at a lower level than in spring. We do not need weight to fish close to the riverbed because, in warm summer water, fish will rise towards the surface to chase and take a lure. Thus we need baits of little weight, monofilament lines of reduced breaking strain, and a fixed-spool reel, the spool of which does not revolve and from which fine lines may be pulled by lightweight baits moving through the air with small momentum. We do not need a wide semicircle of rod swing to cast – a flick is enough – so the rod is suited to use in restricted areas.

There is no doubt that Shimano fixed-spool reels set high standards of excellence. Their Baitrunner Aero GT 5010 comes with two spools, one of which could be loaded with 17-lb monofilament for early-season salmon spinning, and the other with 10–12-lb nylon for summer sea-trout. The reel has a 'baitrunner' lever for worming, which we will be discussing later in this chapter. When engaged, a fish can take line off the reel without restriction; when disengaged, the rear drag system operates.

Line must not be loaded onto the reel spool in the same way as a fly reel. In the latter, the reel and line spool face each other in the same plane; the line spool unwinds as the reel winds and twists do not occur. This does not work with a fixed-spool reel, which would be at right angles to the coil of line to be loaded. If a pencil is put through the centre of the line spool and the spool revolves as it releases line to the reel, many twists will form. The correct method, if you do not have a helper, is to place the spool of new line flat on the floor. You will notice at once, as the reel is wound, whether it has been placed on the floor with the correct side up. If there are twists between the spool and the reel as the reel winds, the spool should be turned over. The coils coming off the spool will then match those going on to the reel. It is important to fill the reel spool to within 2 mm of the lip. If it is overfilled, excess coils of line will come off during casting and a bird's nest will result; if it is underfilled, the line has to lift over the spool lip and long casts cannot be made.

No matter how carefully one loads new line it will be under some twisting tension on the reel. To remove this, tie the end of the line to the *swivel* of a Wye weight (when fishing, the reel line is always tied to the wire loop on the other end of the Wye) and make several long casts downstream into the river; this will remove all tensions as the line untwists.

When fishing, the line will be shortened gradually as baits, swivels and weights are changed, and, some length may be lost when a bait snags on the riverbed. In time, the line level will sink to more than 2 mm below the lip of the drum. When this happens, casting distance will be lost, and the whole line should be replaced. Do not add an extra 10 or 15 yd of nylon by joining the lengths with a blood knot. This may catch in the line guides or reel bail arm, and will always be slightly suspect in strength. The risk is not worthwhile when a new line costs so little.

Braided line is not suited to a fixed-spool reel; only monofilament should be used. The line must be soft and limp without a 'memory' of the windings on the reel spool. I have used a number of lines which went out of production as soon as I was satisfied with their performance. Stren is the exception; it is still on the market and comes in two colours, blue and gold. Either is suitable and the line, being visible, points to the position of the bait as it crosses the river.

For salmon the reel should be loaded with 17 or 14 lb according to your preference, river conditions, and the size of expected fish. If you choose 17 lb, the trace should be 14-lb Maxima Chameleon; if 14 lb is used this should be coupled with a 12-lb Maxima trace. For sea-trout use a 12-lb Stren reel line and 10-lb Maxima trace or 10 lb

A multiplying spinning reel needs a heavy bait and room to swing the rod to start the drum revolving.

Stren and 8 lb Maxima. The trace is 2 ft 6 in or 3 ft of nylon between the reel line and the bait, and is attached to the reel line through a swivel or a weight and swivel, with a tucked half blood knot.

Weights and Swivels

Some anglers tie the spinning bait to the end of the reel line. This is not recommended because the line may become twisted as the bait revolves, even if there is a swivel in the head of the lure, as is the case with Devon Minnows. If the bait is attached to the reel line via a trace of slightly reduced strength, as suggested above, the trace is likely to break before the reel line if the bait snags, and long lengths of line are not left in the river.

The line and trace can be joined using a swivel, a swivel combined with a weight, or an anti-kink ballbearing swivel and plastic vane. This junction is the place to add weight and stop line twists.

The best swivel is the BB, which incorporates ten ballbearings. BBs are sold in packs of three and have an eye at each end. Barrel swivels are also available and are less expensive.

It must be remembered that it is illegal to use weights made of lead if they are less than 1 oz (28 g). This restriction should not cause a problem, as manufacturers now make various styles in lead-free alloys.

The Hillman weight is a ball weight with a wire attachment which can be passed through the top eye of the swivel to which the reel line is tied; the trace is knotted to the lower swivel eye. It is made in various diameters of ball, but being bulky and unstreamlined, it may jam between rocks on the riverbed. It is therefore less suitable than the slim Wye weight.

This is the most popular and convenient type. It has a swivel at one end of its banana shape, to which the trace is attached, and a wire loop at the other, to which the reel line is tied. The bait then spins on the trace attached to the swivel against the 'stop' of the weight. It is available in seven sizes between ⅛ oz (3.5 g) and 1 oz (28 g), but it is not necessary to carry more than two categories for warm-water sea-trout spinning: the ¼ oz (7 g) and ⅜ oz (11 g).

If you add weight at the line/trace junction, be sure it does not exceed the weight of the bait. If it does, the weight will extend beyond the lure in the air as the cast is made, and the bait, travelling behind it, may catch on the line.

Some anglers obtain increased weight by using a heavier lure. In the case of the Devon minnow, this involves wrapping lead wire around the steel wire of the flight (also known as the mount) inside the minnow body. I do not favour this arrangement. The line/trace position is where weight should be added. If the flight is weighted the minnow tends to swim head up and tail down. It is better that the minnow swims on an even keel, as it will do if it swims behind the weight, particularly in the case of wooden Devons.

Spinning Baits

The word 'spinning' is used loosely to cover many artificial baits, some of which, like plugs and Tobies, do not revolve. Some are suited to high, fast-water conditions because they are slim, do not spin too fast and can be retrieved without too much resistance against the water flow when cast downstream. Other baits spin rapidly and are suited to water which is flowing slowly, and to an upstream cast which is reeled back with, but slightly faster than, the current.

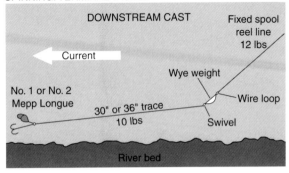

SPINNING: TERMINAL TACKLE

DOWNSTREAM CAST

Current

Fixed spool reel line 12 lbs

Wye weight

Wire loop

No. 1 or No. 2 Mepp Longue

30" or 36" trace 10 lbs

Swivel

River bed

All knots tucked half blood.

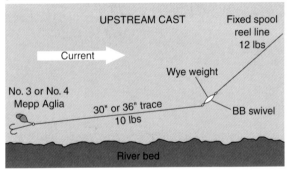

SPINNING: TERMINAL TACKLE

UPSTREAM CAST

Fixed spool reel line 12 lbs

Current

Wye weight

No. 3 or No. 4 Mepp Aglia

30" or 36" trace 10 lbs

BB swivel

River bed

All knots tucked half blood.

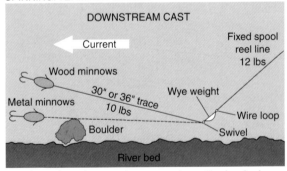

SPINNING: TERMINAL TACKLE

DOWNSTREAM CAST

Current

Fixed spool reel line 12 lbs

Wood minnows

30" or 36" trace 10 lbs

Wye weight

Metal minnows

Wire loop

Boulder

Swivel

River bed

A wooden minnow swims over rocks on the river bed.

Mepp spoons are in my opinion the ideal sea-trout spinning baits. They are available in various colours and shapes from size 00 (1.5 g) to size 5 (13 g). Some patterns are excessively large,

The River Lyd often yields sea-trout in September when one is spinning for salmon with a No 2 Mepp Aglia.

weighing up to 17½ gm. The three most useful designs are the Aglia, the Longue and the Comet Decoree.

Mepp Aglia, the wide oval blade revolves rapidly, and it is suited to slow water flows and upstream casting. Carry three sizes: No 1 and No 2 for clear-water down stream casting; and No 4 for upstream casting in coloured water spate conditions. The size disparity between the three is remarkable but, be assured, the large No 4 cast up the river has brought me many large peal in coloured water in Devon, and a 4-lb sea-trout in the clear waters of the River Test. All three are sold in silver, gold and copper. My choices are silver for the two small sizes, and gold for the No 4.

Beware the treble hook on the smallest sizes of Aglia when large fish are present. If it is of too fine a bendable wire, cut it off and replace it with a No 6 or No 8 bronze round-eye Partridge X1 outbend treble. The spoon and replacement hook can be joined by a Mustad Size 1 oval split ring. Do not use the Partridge X3 needle-eye treble in this position because the split ring cannot move freely in the narrow eye.

The long pointed blade of the **Mepp Longue** revolves closer to the body of the bait than the blade of the Aglia, and thus offers less resistance to water and to the retrieve. In the No 2 copper shade one has an ideal bait for downstream spinning in fast water. The No 1, also in copper, is suited to clearer conditions. Neither fishes well if cast upstream, as they offer insufficient resistance to the flow to revolve attractively unless they are recovered at excessive speed.

The other Mepp model suitable for sea-trout is the **Comet Decoree**, which is ideal for very slow waters as it has a 'fluttering' action. If you stick to

A No 2 Mepp Aglia took this 7-lb sea-trout.

these patterns you will have something to cover most situations.

The **Devon Minnow** is available in wood, plastic or metal, and in all the colours of the spectrum. It is not my choice when spinning specifically for sea-trout in summer, but they have taken heavy peal for me when I have been after salmon in April and May. Sea-trout of 2½ or 3 lb have sufficiently wide mouths to take Devon Minnows of 2–2½ in. For smaller summer fish try a 1½-in Devon in blue and silver in clear water, or brown and gold if the flow is coloured, both in either wood or light plastic. The metal Devon is too heavy for use in shallow water, particularly if it is cast upstream.

The steel wire with a hook at one end and a swivel at the head which passes through the hollow body of the minnow is known as the mount or flight. Examine its construction, for many are poorly designed. It is essential that the wire passes through the ring of an eyed hook and that the ends of the wire, after passing through the swivel and a plastic tulip bead which sits over the treble eye, are crimped together in a metal sleeve. Do not accept spade-end trebles, or flights where the wire is bound to the hook with silk – it may rot.

Slim natural Quill Minnows are available from Sportfish of Winforton, Hereford. They are armed with a single treble in the tail, or with additional flying trebles. A suitable size for sea-trout is 1½ in, but they are also made in 1 and 2 in, in red, brown, green and blue.

The **Irish** or **Lane Minnow**, also from Sportfish, is available in various sizes and colours. It is not as slim as the Quill and, being weighted and offering little water resistance, is better suited to downstream rather than upstream casting.

There is a wide selection of **Toby** types of spoon in many colours, weights and lengths. They are superb attractors, but poor at hooking fish. If I use them, I alter them by adding a second split ring between the treble hook and the Toby blade. This arrangement helps to reduce the risk of the long body levering out the hook.

Worming Rods

As for spinning, the tackle used when worming for sea-trout must be capable of landing salmon. The two methods use different approaches. Worms are usually fished more slowly than artificial baits and on, or close to, the riverbed. This

When spinning for sea-trout a salmon may be taken – carry a 24-in Gye net.

lingering search, either by casting upstream or downstream, allows endless opportunities for snagging. The risk is increased in an upstream cast for then, as the worm is washed downriver, its sinking tendency, together with any weight, causes it to subside into crevices in the riverbed. The same problem occurs, but not to the same extent, in a down-and-across throw, for the river current helps to lift the worm over any riverbed rocks.

The snagging tendency can be partially overcome by the use of a long rod of 12 ft or more. The height of such a rod enables one to keep most of one's line out of the water, and to manoeuvre the

worm around rocks, weeds and other obstructions; it is also better than a short rod when playing fish. The extra length confers two additional advantages. The first is that one can keep back from the river bank; it being essential to remain out of sight of sea-trout, particularly by day. The second is that the long reach often makes it possible to hold a worm in front of a visible fish, as the bait pivots off the rod point if it is pushed out at 90 degrees from the river edge and held in that position.

Two rods are good for worming, both being designed for the presentation of natural baits. The **Hardy Favourite Specialist** is a 12 ft 6 in rod in three sections and, to my mind, is ideal for worming. It does not have the problem of a long butt like salmon spinning rods; Hardy's have equipped it with a movable screw-grip reel mount on the 24-in slim handle. The reel can thus be positioned anywhere on the handle. The rod is also suitable for spinning.

The **Normark Salmon Allrounder** is a 12-ft carbon rod, in three sections, and is less than half the price of the Hardy Favourite Specialist, but it is not possible to alter the position of the reel mount. For the price, it is good value and suitable for worm, shrimp and prawn.

Pupils sometimes ask me whether one can spin with a fly rod and fish the fly with a spinning rod. The answer is no. But worming is different from spinning because a worm is not a heavy object, and a fly rod can be pressed in to service in emergency.

My first sea-trout worming was done in Scotland on a small west-coast river. I was on holiday and had with me a trout rod and a 12-ft double-handed split-cane salmon fly rod. I did not have a long spinning rod or a fixed-spool reel. My spinning outfit at that time was an 8 ft 6 in Glascona rod and a Hardy Elarex multiplying reel, an unsuitable pair, and these had in any case been left at home. The month was July and when I arrived at the section of river I had rented, the river was in spate. The 12-ft rod was pressed into service, a length of nylon, hook and worms tied to the floating fly line and the offering cast into the warm, peaty waters. I was successful, but the worms as often as not objected to being aerialized and, on the back cast, flew off into the bracken behind me. Such a rod may be used in emergency but it is not ideal because you cannot add weight to the worms without the risk of breaking the delicate tip of the rod when casting.

Worming Reels, Weights, Traces and Hooks

The Shimano Baitrunner Aero GT5010 loaded with 12-lb monofilament, as for light spinning, is ideal. Between the line and the 10-lb trace a BB swivel should be knotted. Some weight is usually needed and can be added, in the form of a pierced bullet or barrel weight, to the line above the swivel and resting on it.

As an alternative, lead-free split shot such as Thamesley Sure-Shot in sizes SSG, AAA, 1, 4 and 6 can be added. Another method is not to add a weight, but to put an extra worm on the hook, for all worms are heavier than water.

The hook should be designed so that a worm, threaded up the shank to cover the eye and point, does not slide down to hang from the hook bend. If this happens the shank is exposed. Use hooks in sizes No 2 and No 4 for sea-trout. The Mustad Type 32813 BLN Power Point Worm is round bend, forged and ringed, and has two upward-pointing slices on the black shank, with the point chemically sharpened. The slices, which are just nicks in the metal of the shank, go some way towards preventing the worm sliding down towards the bend. Another suitable sliced Mustad hook is the beakhook, Type 92247. If you do not have a hook designed for worming, take a No 4 single salmon fly and strip off the dressing with your pocket knife, then whip on a bristle of nylon, pointing up towards the eye. The bristle should be whipped along part of its length, the free section being bent slightly out from the shank. Slid up and over the bristle, a worm cannot slide down.

Worms

The best kind of worm is a large one; fish them two at a time. They may be purchased, but it is better to catch your own on warm damp nights on a lawn or other short grass such as golf course or cricket pitch. They are very quick to retreat

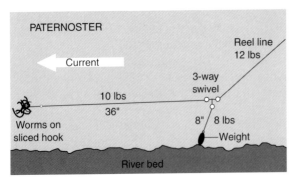

All knots tucked half blood.

A bunch of worms covers the hook point and is a succulent mouthful.

into their holes and, when grabbed, their protruding setae enable them to cling to the hole beneath the surface. If steady pressure is maintained they ultimately let go. Alternatively, you will find a good supply when you are digging your garden!

Worms can be stored for several weeks in a bucket of damp moss kept in a cool, dark place, preferably with an inch or two of earth in the bottom. Some people feed them with lettuce leaves or other vegetable matter, which rots into the moss.

CHAPTER 5

Spinning and Worming Tactics

Casting

It is not unusual to see an angler who is about to cast a spinning bait facing the river whilst standing upright on the river bank, the rod almost vertical, but slightly behind his head, with the bait hanging down from the tip. He casts, zipping the rod tip forward over his head, the bait arcs up into the air, crosses the river, and drops almost vertically into the water close to the far bank – a splendid exhibition of power and accuracy provided there are no fish to be scared in the river, and no trees overhanging the water on the far side through which the bait can drop.

It would be better to wade beneath the bank or kneel on it, or cut one's silhouette by casting from in front of a bush. An overhead cast makes for distance and accuracy and is fine on treeless, open rivers if one kneels, but is impossible on waters enclosed in a tunnel of trees, and the bait is likely to catch in the branches of trees on the other bank if they spread out over the water. In such places the flight of the bait should be in as flat a trajectory as possible. The rod should start the cast from a position close to the horizontal and finish in the same plane. The bait will then shoot across the river a few feet above the water, passing beneath any overhanging branches – unless they are very close to the water surface. The trace should not be more than 3 ft in length, preferably 2 ft 6 in; if it is longer, the rod tip will have to start the cast from a high position slightly behind you to avoid the bait dragging on the ground at the

start of the cast. And if you start the throw with the rod tip high, the trajectory is likely to be 'up and over', with the risk of the bait dropping through any branches on the opposite bank as it descends.

You should be able to cast with the rod to the right or left of your body at the start of the movement. If you are right-handed and casting with the rod to the right, your right hand should be close to and slightly in front of the reel in order to hold the line over your forefinger with the bail arm open, and your left hand should rest on the butt as a pivot, with the butt passing across your body.

If you are right-handed but casting with the rod starting to the left of your body (perhaps because there is a tree immediately to your right), your right hand takes the same position in front of the reel, but the length of the butt will lie under your right forearm. In that position you can gain extra power for this backhanded throw if your left forearm crosses your body to grip and steady the end of the rod butt under your right forearm.

It is not necessary to make a wide sweep of the rod when indeed, such a sweep makes casting difficult to be accurate. Moreover, you will be doing much of the work which should be done by the top section of the rod. A sharp flick of the top section, with little whole-rod movement, provides accuracy and a fast, flat trajectory of the bait.

Releasing Snagged Baits

A bait snagged beneath the water surface can usually be released without any risk. A minnow and weight caught in a tree on the far side of the river is a different matter, for a giant catapult has been created, with the elastic monofilament line, a weighted bait, a tree branch under tension, and you as the target.

If you cannot cross the river, accept that the bait is likely to be lost and proceed as follows. Go 15 yd away from your bank into the adjacent field, wrap a handkerchief around your hand, and over this take two turns of the line. Turn your back on the river, put your head down behind your upturned collar and continue to walk away until the increasing tension breaks the trace. The weight will fly across the river and smack into the earth, not you. If you do not go far enough from the river the weight, or the bait if it comes free, may hit you on the back or the back of your legs. There is a hole in the shoulder of one of my waxed jackets made by a catapulted Wye weight.

It is likely that the trace will break before the reel line, as it is weaker, although the reel line may break at the tucked half blood knot joining it to the swivel or Wye weight, because these knots reduce the breaking strain of nylon by 15 per cent. A single turn, the equivalent of a wind knot in a fly cast, reduces the strength by 50 per cent, so do not tolerate any other knots in your monofilament.

If a bait becomes caught on some object close to or on the riverbed downstream of your position do not pull straight away. It is better to open the reel bail arm and allow 20 yd of line to be washed in a loop below the bait, then close the bail arm and sweep the rod up in a sharp movement. The line downstream of the stuck bait may well pluck it free. If this does not work, go downstream and pull from various angles. The bait may come free, but with one hook of the treble bent slightly open. Sometimes one has to pull until the trace

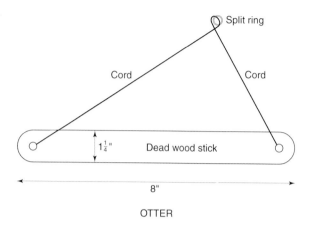

OTTER

breaks. Some anglers use an 'otter' (see drawing), sliding this down the line to jiggle the bait from above. This may work, but it causes considerable disturbance to the river and to any fish in the vicinity. If one of the points of a treble has opened after catching on an obstruction, it is weakened and should be replaced.

Upstream and Downstream Casting

A sea-trout entering the river in May or June has five or six months to spend in fresh water before it is time to spawn in the headwaters. If the redding area is 20, 30 or even 40 miles upstream, the fish could reach it in a week of swimming, or it could take several weeks or even months. During this time it has nothing to do other than exist. It takes no food on a regular basis; it just rests quiescent with perhaps a short period of exercise – a leap or two – at dawn and dusk. The fish is not greatly interested in anything you do unless it decides to seek safer quarters if you show yourself outlined against the sky.

Then things change; the barometer registers a fall in pressure, and it rains. High in the hills the clouds release their burden, the streamlets, brooks and runnels fill, a spate starts to run down the valley and the sea-trout stirs. The coming of new, stained, tasty water stimulates it. Then suddenly, in its tensed state, it sees an extraordinary

Four September sea-trout and one salmon all took a No 4 Mepp Aglia cast upstream.

whirring thing, your No 4 Mepp Aglia swimming and flashing on a curving path down the river. It will soon be gone; there is just a fleeting moment to grab it as it passes and your rod arcs as the line tightens.

An upstream cast with a large Mepp Aglia is rewarding in warm, coloured water at the start of a spate, at its peak if it is not a flood and, best of all, as it starts to drop and clear. One of the most productive afternoons on my beat was in September when a spate arrived after drought. We took one salmon, lost a grilse, and landed four sea-trout to a total of 17 lb, all on a No 4 Mepp Aglia cast upstream as the spate passed its peak and the water began to clear.

Whether a spate produces good fishing depends to some extent on the length of the dry period before the arrival of rain. If there has been a drought of several weeks or two or three months, the first spate is likely to be unfishable. The water will be dark and heavily contaminated with peat if it is running off moorland, or clay or sandstone if the course is through agricultural land. A great deal of rubbish will come down. I have even seen a dead and distended cow float through my beat with all four legs pointing to the sky. In Scotland there will be flotillas of empty whisky bottles. The next spate, if it arrives within a week or ten days, will provide better fishing in cleaner water.

A salmon and sea-trout ladder in high water.

The same ladder in low water when it is best to fish the fly at night.

An upstream cast is not so productive in clear water when there is not the excitement of rain, but it still yields an occasional peal. The lure should be smaller, a No 1 or No 2 Mepp Aglia, again with a swift retrieve. Chances are improved if the day is cloudy and there is a strong wind to ruffle the surface of the water. Even so, peal will be seen to follow the revolving bait until you run out of water and have to lift out; the fish then veer off without taking.

An upstream cast is rarely successful for salmon or sea-trout unless the water is warm. Happily it almost always is warm when one is fishing for peal, for they enter the river in late spring and throughout the summer. I have not caught salmon or sea-trout with an upstream throw before the third week in April, and they do not often come to my upstream Mepp until June.

The Mepp Longue can be used for downstream casting in sizes No 1 and No 2, but it does not spin sufficiently fast for an upstream cast which is retrieved with the current. The best places to use a Longue are the necks of pools where the current is compressed and thus flows faster than in wider sections of the river. A downstream throw is rarely fruitful unless there is an increase in water flow following rain.

Of course, as in fishing a fly, where you find your fish will depend on the height of the water. In night, fly-fishing in low water the tails of the pools are usually productive, and the necks less so. By day, in a falling but still high river, the tails of the pools will still be the best places, as they are less turbulent than the necks. There will also be high-water resting places that would not be occupied, and might even be dry, when the river is back to its bare bones. These high-water lies are usually to the side of main currents, in the middle of slower pools and in long smooth glides. They are not in the fast, rough stickles.

Worming

I am not an authority on fishing the worm for sea-trout, as it is not allowed on my home river; the prohibition also applies to salmon. The worm has

This pipe is the author's water-level gauge. As shown, the level is ideal for fishing the fly at night. If it is halfway up the pipe it is better to fish by day on a joint salmon/sea-trout expedition.

also been banned on the River Test, rightly so in my view as migratory fish runs have declined and every effort is being made to restore populations. I mention salmon because, if you fish the worm for sea-trout you will catch all manner of fish, including eels. A worm is not selective and is very effective if you can put up with finding, storing, carrying and looking after a creature which must be kept moist, cool and out of the sun, and which dies quickly on the hook. As with spinning, if you are truly addicted you will carry more tackle as you rattle your way along the river bank than when fishing the fly: weights, spools of nylon, various hooks, shots, swivels, anti-kink vanes and sometimes even floats – and, of course, worms in tins and buckets.

I have occasionally been on a West Country river where worms are allowed, and I have found the scene depressing. On the edge of each reasonable pool sits an angler watching a line which slants down into the depths, both the angler and his outfit quite static. Once, after I had watched for a considerable time, one angler pulled his bait out of the water. On the end of the line was a large fishmonger's prawn *and* two lobworms – this on a river famed for its sea-trout runs!

I do not think one should be categorically opposed to worming, but if it is allowed it should not be overdone. It should rather be regarded as a skilled method to be pressed into service when a fish is desperately needed for the table and river conditions are unsuitable for spinning or fly-fishing. To my mind this means in times of heavy, warm summer water of very poor clarity.

Upstream worming is difficult, as worms and weights are easily snagged around obstructions, but keep the rod tip high and recover line at the same speed as that of the worm drifting down towards you. The downstream throw will require a little more weight to keep the worm close to the bed of the river – you are unlikely to catch sea-trout, or anything else, if the worm is swept across the river close to the surface. The downstream method has the advantage that the

passage of the worm may be slow as you pay out line, and the bait will precede line, swivel and weight or split shot. The paternoster system allows the bait to be fished close to the riverbed slowly and with the worm drifting downstream ahead of the line, swivel and weight (see drawing).

At all times, and whatever your method, keep the monofilament line between the fingers of the hand which is not holding the rod. Try to feel and imagine the passage of the worm as you assist it to circumvent obstructions whilst keeping it close to the riverbed. A tweak signifies interest by a fish – do nothing. There should be several tweaks, perhaps a firm pull, but pause for a few seconds before lifting the rod tip to secure the fish.

If you find yourself in Wales (home of the worm) or Scotland without a spinning or bait rod but with a 10-ft or 11-ft fly rod, you can, if you have had the foresight to pack a fixed-spool reel or a trotting reel, fish the worm successfully. To the end of the reel line tie a stripped salmon fly hook as described in Chapter 4. Some weight is probably needed; you can use a sliver of lead from a roof flashing or an old lead water pipe, or use the lead foil covering the cork of a wine bottle. (Whether these come within the 28-g rule, not being fishing weights, I do not know.) Draw several pulls of line off the reel, cast into the river and then recover line by drawing in over the index finger of the hand on the rod butt. This 'handing' of the line is sensitive in detecting nibbles. If you wind in by the reel you cannot feel a take.

An alternative to the fixed-spool reel is the trotting reel loaded with monofilament or fine braided terylene. These reels are of large diameter – 4–4½ in is normal – friction free when rotating as the line goes out, and with an audible drag when one is playing a fish. They are to be preferred to a fly reel and fly line.

If you have neither fixed-spool nor a trotting reel, a fly reel and line is a substitute, but a poor one by comparison, as the line is difficult to shoot and cast without the speed of casting causing the worms to fly off the hook. A single-handed fly rod of 10 or 11 ft is much better than a 12-ft double-handed rod, which is likely to be too heavy to be manipulated with one hand. I have taken several grilse, sea-trout and finnock with the fly-rod/worm method. It is entertaining and can be successful, for a worm can almost always be found under a stone. The problem in Scotland is not catching fish, but withstanding the onslaught of midges.

CHAPTER 6

Fly-Fishing by Day

It is no good imagining that you are regularly going to take many sea-trout from a river, by day on a fly, unless it is in a spate. It just will not happen. There is no alternative to fishing at night if you want a regular supply for the table. But a loch is a different matter. You can make a good catch by day on a windy loch in Scotland, unless the sea-lice are decimating the finnock and the runs are slowly dying. This is the case on Scottish west-coast rivers and lochs due, I believe, to the proximity of salmon farms.

In Rivers

On the whole, fly-fishing by day is frustrating and tantalizing when the river is low and clear and the surface is unruffled by wind. From the bank, or high in the branches of a tree, you search the pools through polarized spectacles, but it takes practice to discern shoals of peal. Novices can stare for hours at the river where there is a group of resting fish without seeing them. They are amazed when I point out the flicker of a silver flank, or the white lips of a yawning peal. But once they have found the knack of looking through the water skin for the shadows of fish on the riverbed, their excitement rises: 'Why can't we catch them, Charles?', to which I have to reply, 'Because they are extremely shy and unlikely to respond to our attentions'.

Posting them up a tree to watch, I take a 5X knotless tapered leader with a 3-lb point, knot on a No 18 Black Gnat or a No 14 Pheasant Tail Nymph dressed with fine copper wire to make it sink, whichever takes my fancy at the time, and creep downstream of the shoal. The upstream cast must be accurate. If the fly line enters the window of a fish, rather than just the fly and leader point, they will be off. If the fly line remains downstream and unseen, the result is usually the same, except that the shoal moves forward a yard, still close to the riverbed. If I persist, they swim away and disappear into deep water.

This is not to say that peal do not take natural flies off the river surface from time to time; they do, but they rarely take an artificial. I have watched both shoals and individual fish whilst lying on the bank. Very occasionally one will be seen to rise to sip a natural fly – a sedge, midge pupa, olive or Crane fly – but I may have to wait all day. Their way is so different from that of small brown trout, which are active 1 ft or 6 in below the surface, swinging from side to side, accepting midge pupae, always feeding, always on the lookout for a sustaining morsel. One only has to open the stomach of one of those small browns to find a compressed black mass of nymphs, duns, stone-fly creepers, and many tiny black beetles if one is on a heather moor. In the stomach of a sea-trout, there is almost always nothing. So do not expect to catch much in calm, low-water conditions by day.

Having said that, consider the following diary entries:

13 August 1987. Three school peal. Best 1 lb. No 8 Black Lure and tandem Black Lure. Bryan and self. Fine warm night. Three-quarter moon. Caught in a mist which came up. Unusually, inside one fish were many stonefly creepers, some nymphs and a wasp.

18 August 1987. Three school peal. Two fish empty. One stuffed with stonefly creepers, midge pupae and a black beetle.

As those school peal were caught soon after sunset, their stomachs must have been filled during the day. The most numerous creatures in them, when I washed the contents apart in a saucer at the kitchen sink the next morning, were the stonefly nymphs. These are not free swimmers like nymphs of the order *Ephemeroptera*; they creep. Their habitat is the underwater sides of boulders and the riverbed. So if you want to try for school peal in a river by day, other than by dapping or dibbling in a wind, that is the level at which your offering should be – deep. This is best achieved by a fine long leader of 12 ft, and a weighted small nymph such as Sawyer's Killer Bug or a copper-wired Pheasant Tail.

Fast, rippling streamy water offers a better chance, even in low, clear conditions and without wind, but it is only very slightly better. Sometimes, perhaps once or twice in a season, when one is fishing a 5X leader and dry fly for brown trout in summer, a peal may have a go. One is aware that it is a sea-trout from the silver flank which flashes underwater and the fact that it is larger than the native brownies, rather than from identification on the bank, as they usually break the nylon under a rock.

An upstream wind to ruffle the surface improves the odds of catching a fish, but only very slightly if the water is low and clear. The ripples do disguise the line and leader, and there is a slim chance with a wet fly thrown upstream and stripped back fast, as with upstream spinning. There is almost no chance in low, calm sunlit water with a downstream wet fly.

The situation alters dramatically in a spate. A good catch may be had by day in stained water, even without a wind, if one fishes in the right places as the water level starts to fall yet retains some colour. There are three such areas in the water I frequent which regularly yield fish. These are lies where I catch fish at night in low water. In a spate the depth is increased by about 12 in. Doubtless the extra depth imparts a feeling of security, the coloured water is a slight shield against the light of day and the line of shallow rock across the tails of the pools acts as a buttress against which sea-trout rest whilst the main flow passes over their heads. Sometimes they will be just below the neck of a pool, just to the side of the run-in and resting with their flanks against the edge rock. This is not as productive as the wide tail, but it is always worth a few casts in passing, for fish are bound, sooner or later, to pass through as they migrate up the river.

Having decided on the lies to be fished, use your standard night tackle, a leader tapered to an 8-lb point and a large fly. The No 8 Black Lure does well, or a 1-in Alexandra Tube. Try a cast upstream into the deeper water whilst standing in the tail of a pool, and then strip back faster than the flow; the fly retrieved in a curving swim across the river is always more attractive than a straight recovery. This is done by casting up and across the current at 45 degrees from your bank. The fly starts to return almost straight down the river then, as the current takes hold of the line it sweeps across to you, finishing in a curve at 45 degrees downstream. This tactic should also be used when a boat is being rowed rather than drifting. The cast, at right angles to the path of the boat, is taken in the final moments as the fly curves to follow the path of the boat. A further application is the backed up salmon cast in which one pitches one's fly across the river immediately opposite one's position, takes two or three steps upstream and recovers the fly in a pronounced curve. I once rose and failed to

This 3 lb 10 oz peal took a 1-in Black Dart tube fly in a spate . . .

. . . in this place whilst the author fished for salmon.

attract six out of seven salmon in a morning whilst fishing conventionally down 2 miles of river; fly changes made no difference. After lunch I backed-up the same pools, starting at each tail. I had two rises and took two salmon.

Over the years many sea-trout have come my way whilst I have been after salmon. The majority have been good-sized fish of 2, 3 or 4 lb and my daughter had one of 7 lb. The remarkable thing is that they seem to prefer the substantial salmon tube flies which I started to fish in spates in the late 1970s. Before then, when I was in my No 6 single Low-water Hairy Mary phase, they would have nothing to do with the fly in high or low water, although I landed many salmon. Beneath the surface, then, they seem to like a good mouthful. I remember one exception in the 1950s when I was camped beside the river. A small peal of about 1½ lb took the small fine-wired hook one morning. I put it in my tent to bake in the fire that night for supper, but when I returned in the evening it was gone – and that was before there were many mink in Devon.

On the subject of mink, a man I was teaching caught a grilse one morning. Not wishing to carry the fish throughout the day we hid it under a gorse bush intending to retrieve it at the end of the day. I waited in the car, high above the valley, and at about 6.00 pm he appeared, without the fish, which he could not find. Far from pleased at what I thought was his poor memory of the hiding place, I went down the hill. The fish was not where it had been hidden, but 25 yd away, hidden in a clump of bracken with the head chewed off. Since then I always carry my fish or string them up in a tree.

If one fishes two flies, sea-trout will occasionally take a small treble dibbled over the water surface as a dropper. My choice for this is a short-shanked shrimp fly dressed on a No 12 Partridge X2B, or a short-shanked double. If these hooks are not available, a Partridge X1 No 10 black out-point treble may be used, with the dressing applied straight onto the short shank. It is an advantage that my standard salmon fly rod in summer is either a 12-ft Hardy graphite or a 13-ft Norboron. Both of these enable me to dribble the dropper over the rough neck of a pool whilst keeping back from the water, and to start the skittering when the flies are still some way from my position. There is a risk when fishing two flies that the free fly will catch in weed or on a rock or sunked branch or root and pull the other one out of the fish.

Attaching the dropper is simple. Cut the plain untapered leader of 12 or 15 lb 1 yd down from the line/leader junction and join the pieces with a blood knot but leave one end 4–5 in long to form the dropper. The long end should be the continuation of the top section to give security when playing a fish on the dropper. This dropper fly has to be attached with a tucked half blood in this position, as there is insufficient length of nylon for a two-turn Turle.

I have occasionally had salmon follow a skidding point fly fished alone without a dropper. This has happened by chance when a strong upstream wind has caught hold of the fly line and blown it up the river, causing it to drag the single tube across the water surface. More than once an open mouth has followed but not quite caught the fly before the back cast lifted it into the air. This experience is leading me to investigate use of the floss blow line for sea-trout on a river.

As I have said, the sea-trout is a migratory brown trout. In the first half of the nineteenth century casting a fly for trout was not possible; it only became so with the arrival of dressed fly lines and short fly rods of about 10 ft capable of being cast with one hand. Before that the method of fly fishing was by 'blowing'. This required a long rod of about 18 ft or more. A light undressed line carried the fly out in the wind over the water where dipped onto the water surface. If there was no wind, one either did not fish or found a companion to 'cross line'. This involved one person on each side of the river, each with a long

Lara Bingham playing a 7-lb peal . . .

. . . and the author landing the fish.

rod, with a line crossing the river between the two and a fly suspended in midstream, and no doubt resulted in confusion, shouting and lost tempers on hot days. Various flies were used, including the Father Long-legs. If one examines prints of the River Test valley in the 1830s, one can see that there are few trees; they were cut down to allow plenty of wind for the blow line.

The practice and the results of blowing are well documented. The Rev Richard Durnford, who was appointed rector of Chilbolton on the Test in 1806, was an avid fisherman and he kept a diary of his outings, including the following:

> 23 May 1811, wind WSW, quite sufficient, sun brighter. Began at Garrison at 12 o'clock. No fly on the water, fish quiet. Tried several kinds of natural flies, Father Long-legs and such others as could be caught. Observed a fish come several times to a Father Long-legs but would not take it. Tried him with a Blue-bottle, which he took

immediately. Caught also another fish with the same fly, and hooked a third – all in very shallow water.

As we know, when dapping on a loch the blow line depends on wind to carry out the fly. Durnford recorded wind strength with care in the following categories: sufficient, quite sufficient, strong, whistling and very violent.

As one becomes older, there is a strong inclination to stop stumbling around in the dark and seek one's sport in daylight hours. My home is on Dartmoor where much of the fishing is done 1,000 ft above the sea. Wind? At times it drives me mad. In fact, as the prevailing south-westerlies blow down the river, frustrating my upstream dry fly for trout, there are moments when it is more than I can stand. Unlike the Test, where Durnford fished, the river is easily forded in thigh boots if one knows the time-honoured places. 'Blowing' could thus be done from

Dapping on the river.

either side, or up or down whilst standing in the river; I would not be limited to one side as Durnford was.

With visions of the 'up and over, head and tail' rises to dapped Daddies, Loch Ordies and other bumbly flies experienced on lochs, I wondered, why not on a river? The equipment is not expensive: Shakespeare market a 17-ft telescopic dapping rod for under £40, and 40 yd of dapping floss costs less than £5. I therefore decided recently to give dapping a try.

I spent two afternoons on the left bank of the River Dart with a north-west wind blowing out across the river. The month was July, but there were not many sea-trout high up on Dartmoor, and there were problems with the floss line catching on thorn bushes. Although I did not catch a sea-trout, two fish boiled at the fly. The wind, according to Durnford's classification, was 'quite sufficient'.

Further experimentation may bring success. It seems to me that a wind in the 'strong' category is needed to disturb the water surface to a wave, thus preventing the rod being seen. In a loch the boat drifts downwind and the dapped fly is constantly moving over new water. In a river this is not the case, and the risk of a long rod being seen is greater. In my travels to other rivers I have heard of one angler who caught sea-trout by dapping on the Border Esk, so there is room for further trials with a strong wind in a helpful direction.

Boat Fishing on Lochs

A boat is an uncomfortable floating platform from which to fish. The problems of a numb bottom and twisted spine can be avoided by buying an extending boat seat which fits across the width of the boat and rests on the gunwales. Less expensive is a cushion on a thwart, but this does not enable you to command the water from the increased height provided by a boat seat. If you are buying a cushion, get one which blows up

into a ring and will act as an emergency life-saver which can be thrown to someone in the water. Height in a seat is desirable, as it is dangerous to stand whilst casting as you may be tipped out of the boat in rough weather. One is also more visible to fish.

Safety should be a prime consideration. On wide Scottish lochs a gale may blow up rapidly, with the result that the boat sometimes has to be beached, and the anglers are forced to walk home. Study weather forecasts and put a lifejacket on over your clothes at the start of the day.

The boatman is the key to success. He must be enthusiastic, which can be difficult when the loch is calm, the sun high in a cloudless sky and his rods are inconsiderate or incompetent casters. I have acted as boatman to novice flyfishers on a number of occasions, and I am no stranger to the turned-up collar, pulled-down hat and mittens protecting the backs of my hands on the oars as flies whip overhead. Hotel boatmen are usually locals who know their lochs intimately: when to hurry the boat over deep areas which do not hold fish, slow it over shallow, productive banks and idle around a rock that is usually home to a good fish.

For dapping, the reel on the 17-ft rod should be filled with braided or monofilament 20-lb backing, on top of which is about 15 yd of floss blow line. To ensure that the reel is full it may be necessary to wind some old fly line on to the drum beneath the backing and floss, both of which are thin and do not take up much room. To the end of the floss knot about 3 ft of 8-lb monofilament with a fly tied on. The essential weather factor is the wind; if it is too strong, the fly will be blown off the water even if you lower the tip of the dapping rod; if it is not strong enough, it will not carry the fly out, enabling it to dance across the water.

Dapping flies should be fat and bumbly, on single lightweight hooks of about size No 8. The pattern and colour do not matter to any great extent as they are seen from below in silhouette

Equipment for dapping with an 18-ft telescopic rod. From left to right: dapping flies, floss line on fly reel, 8-lb Maxima Chameleon for 4-ft leader, Supafloat to waterproof the fly, Mucilin to waterproof the fly, hood to strap over the line guides when the rod is closed.

against the sky: Loch Ordie, Fore and Aft, and Blue Zulu are suitable. The fly must be water-proofed in Gink or Supafloat, and a smear of solid Mucilin will increase buoyancy. The yard of nylon on which the fly is suspended need not be greased, as it should not rest upon the water – just the fly is allowed to touch the waves. The fishing is simple: the floss is drawn up through the rod rings and allowed to stream out in the wind ahead of the boat. Raising or lowering the tip of the rod and swinging it from side to side allows the fly to cover a wide arc of water at variable distances from the boat.

All your preparations and care can come to nothing if the rod is raised too soon when a fish comes up to take the fly. Let the fish curve over and its tail disappear beneath the waves – that is your moment.

Dapping all day is a strain on the eyes, which must be focused constantly on the fly. It is there-fore a relief to fish a wet fly for a while. If you are sharing a boat, one angler could dap and the other fish wet, swapping methods from time to time. A change always brings new impetus.

A single-handed rod of 10 or 11 ft in carbon fibre or Boron is ideal, particularly if it has an easy action and takes a No 6 line. There is no need for a tip-action AFTM No 7/8 rod capable of cutting

into the wind, as casts are made downwind of the boat in the direction of the drift, or across the wind to either side. It is usual to fish a floating line, but take a slow sinker or sink-tip in addition.

Use a home-made monofilament leader in three sections – 3 ft of 20 lb, 3 or 4 ft of 15 or 13 lb and 4 ft of 8 lb – with droppers at the two junctions. I usually attach the top fly, normally called the bob, with a short length of 8-lb nylon, as the 20-lb top section nylon is too thick for the eyes of trout-sized flies and too stiff to allow the fly to work in the water. The bob suspension is made by tying a tucked half blood knot of the 8-lb monofilament against the 20-lb nylon and sliding it down to rest on the 20/15 blood knot. An alternative method uses a water knot; the 15- or 13-lb middle section, pointing up, is the bob extension.

As to flies, you will not go far wrong with Peter Ross, Mallard & Claret or Black Pennell for the point fly and dropper, probably in sizes No 8, No 10 and No 12, depending on the colour of the water and the size of the waves. For the bob fly, which could be greased, try a Zulu.

If two people are fishing from one boat with the boatman in between it would be ideal, though rare, if one is right handed and the other left handed, as they are then able to cast with the rod hand over the bow and the stern. If both cast with the same hand, fishing is not so easy and each should watch the other to ensure that back casts are taken in turn and do not meet in the air behind the boat.

If there is no boatman it makes for good fishing if one person takes the oars and the other fishes, changing over every hour. Care should be taken when moving in the boat not to thump on the bottom boards, as this causes vibrations which will be transmitted to the fish. This is a particular problem with modern glass-fibre boats, which are noisy conveyances compared with the wooden rowing boats of 30 or 40 years ago.

When fishing the wet fly remember that a curved retrieve is more attractive than a cast made and recovered in a straight line ahead of the boat. Cast to either side and, by swinging the rod tip forward, induce a curve as the line approaches the moment of lift-off, at the same time raising the rod point to cause the bob and then the dropper to drag across the surface. If the cast is made across the wind the flies will straighten in a curve behind and parallel to the path of the boat. This method is most effective, but the back cast must be made with extreme care to avoid hitting the boatman and your fishing companion, it is probably safer to use it when only one rod is fishing and the other is at the oars. With a long single-handed rod a single Spey cast will safely place the fly away to the side of the line of drift of the boat without any risk to the other occupants.

CHAPTER 7

Ten Rivers and a Loch

The Taw, North Devon

The Taw rises on Dartmoor above Sticklepath, then flows north-west to a joint estuary with the river Torridge north of Bideford, at Appledore. It has a fine run of sea-trout, being one of the top four peal rivers in the South West, a distinction shared with the Camel, the Fowey and the Teign, closely followed by the Dart. It usually produces twice the rod catch of its sister river, the Torridge.

I was fortunate in meeting the Environment Agency bailiff for the Taw, Jeremy Boyd, who gave a satisfactory report on the care of the river and measures to protect and encourage runs of migratory fish. These measures have halted and reversed the reductions in salmon and sea-trout populations and rod catches on the Taw and the Torridge, particularly the latter, caused by pollution, disease, and overnetting in the estuary. The decline was noticeable from the early 1980s.

Roddy Rae casting above King Bridge. At night a roll-cast is needed to avoid the trees to the rear.

Roll-casting on the Taw. Sea-trout lie at night under the trees.

To assist in the restoration of migratory fish runs, no netting was allowed for five years up to and including 1995. Net licences were issued for 1996, but reduced from 36 to 14; in 1997 it is proposed that there be a shortened net season, and licences be further reduced to 7, this subject to a public enquiry.

There were no rod catch limits for peal in 1996, but there will be a limit of 40 peal per rod for the season in 1997, and ten in one week, again subject to the public enquiry. Additionally, spinning on the river has been prohibited after the end of April; in 1997 fly fishing will be the only method allowed after 31 March for both salmon and sea-trout. Natural bait fishing is not allowed. The open rod seasons on Taw are: salmon, 1 March–30 September; sea-trout, 15 March–30 September.

Spawning is good in the tributaries, which are kept clean, and with loose gravel, by the use of high-pressure water hoses and, in accessible sites, by JCB diggers. The cleaning of gravel beds is necessary because of increased silt deposition in the last 30 years following more efficient land drainage. The present drainage into the Taw has given the river almost the characteristics of a spate river, with a reduced number of fishing days on a falling river before the water is back to a low level. Increased silt deposition is most noticeable on the lower sections, where the course is through agricultural land. The moorland spawning areas are less silted, but the problem there is compacted gravel, which has to be loosened to enable the fish to cut redds. The best spawning areas of good gravel are downstream of North Tawton weir. Not only are the spawning areas kept clean and sources of pollution detected, but the water is sampled frequently, often weekly in many areas. Checks are made regularly on licensed discharges, including those from sewage treatment works.

Juvenile fish populations are monitored every four years by electro-survey on 104 sites on the tributaries and the main river. The surveys are now carried out without stop nets and in one single pass instead of three. This slightly reduced detection level allows a team to cover three sites per day. The previous three-pass surveys were time-consuming and could no longer be funded on reduced government grants.

Sea-trout spawning starts on the river in early November, about two weeks before salmon commence digging their redds. Jeremy notices that brown trout sometimes fertilize the ova of sea-trout, and that peal redds tend to be towards the edge of a stream. In that position they are more liable to dry out than salmon redds, which are in deeper water in the middle of a tributary.

Two miles north of the Junction Pool, the meeting place of the rivers Taw and Mole, is the High Bullen Hotel, where I met Chris Taylor, the hotel estate and fishery manager, and Roddy Rae of the Half Stone Sporting Agency, which has access to the hotel waters.

The hotel owns, rents, and has day rods on many miles of double- and single-bank fishing on the Taw. These stretch from New Bridge, the first fishery above the tide, upstream almost to Umberleigh on the 4½ miles of right-bank Hall Estate waters. I took a number of salmon in the 1970s from Dobb's and Horestones pools whilst fishing the left bank, and these pools are also good for sea-trout. There is an arrangement on 1 mile of double-bank fishing at Weirmarsh which is 2 miles upstream of Umberleigh. This beat had yielded in the region of 50 salmon in the 1996 season up to the time of my visit in July.

The hotel also has four beats on the River Mole, the main tributary of the Taw. These beats provide trout, sea-trout and salmon fishing, and clear quickly after a spate, becoming fishable before the Taw has changed colour from spate brown to a tinge of green. I have often hung over Umberleigh Bridge hoping for this colour change, which foretells the fishable clarity to come. The combination of the Taw and the Mole is a good one for the angler: when the Taw is overful and coloured, the Mole may have cleared; when the Mole is too low in summer, the Taw has sufficient water.

There are no obstructions on the Taw to prevent sea-trout and salmon reaching the Junction Pool.

In consequence, fish with tailed sea-lice can reach that pool from the sea within approximately 24 hours of passing under New Bridge. These runs are particularly noticeable after the spring tides of full moons. There is an obstruction, Head Weir, on the Mole above the Junction Pool, which prevents fish running the river if the water is low, despite the presence of a fish pass.

Large sea-trout start to be caught on the Mole in mid-April by rods spinning for salmon. In 1996 peal of 7½ and 10 lb were taken from the Mole as high upstream as George Nympton. Sea-trout in the Taw are of a good size, averaging 3 lb before the arrival of school peal. Chris lost a very large peal on the Mole in early June, taking off most of his backing and breaking the leader. The next night he took a 6½-lb peal on a No 12 double Butcher on 10-lb nylon. It had 14 scales between the adipose fin and the lateral line. His companion that night on the Lenton Beat took a sea-trout of 4 lb.

Otters are common on the river. Both Chris and Roddy have seen them swim through sea-trout pools at dusk, and then caught fish.

The flies used are those which are effective on many rivers: Silver Stoat's Tail and Alexandra. Some are fished as tubes, others as singles. Short-taking peal are a problem, as they are on all rivers. Roddy has gone some way towards solving this frustrating problem. His fly is comprised of two No 14 or No 16 trebles in tandem. These are joined by ¼ or ½ in of monofilament covered by silver Mylar tubing. The dressing is in the Silver Stoat's Tail or Alexandra style.

A local fly, the Loxy, is of the same construction as my Burglar: a treble behind a streamer shank of which the hook of the single has been cut off at the bend. The dressing is as for a Silver Stoat. Local fishermen are not known to use Beta lights or luminous strip on their sea-trout flies.

The Taw passes through agricultural land for many miles. In summer the water tends to be more coloured and opaque than the flow in moorland rivers, owing to algae. This limitation on clarity requires a larger fly, even a No 6 single, as

Fertilizer bags protect rubber thigh boots from barbed wire.

is the case on the Tamar, which also runs through cultivated farmland. The Mole flows off Exmoor through meadowland. Because there is little cultivation, it clears quickly after a spate, has little algae in summer, and warrants a smaller fly.

In moonlight Roddy also uses the Teign Ghost, described later in this chapter, off a floating fly line but, in deep pools where it will not snag the riverbed, a sinking braided leader can be used. To the 5-ft braided leader is added a tippet of 5–8-lb breaking strain nylon, between 3 and 5 ft in length. In July and August, in low water, the 5-lb point comes into use, and it is adequate to land the majority of fish. Surface lures are also fished at night, usually Black or White Muddlers stripped across the surface. The leader would be a floating braid and ungreased 4-ft monofilament tippet.

High Bullen has a selection of rods and tackle for hire to hotel guests, and can supply waders. Much of the Mole sea-trout fishing is done from in the river whilst wearing chest waders; the Taw is mainly fishable from the bank, or in thigh boots. Chris meets fishing guests at 9.00 am each morning in the bar to discuss their needs and to supply flies, leaders and other items.

When fishing the Taw, Roddy uses an 8- or 9-ft Bruce & Walker Powerlite rod, a No 6 JLH Ultralite reel of 3¼-in diameter loaded with an AFTM No 5 white floating line. His net is 20-in in diameter with a metal ring.

The Environment Agency issues Jeremy Boyd with a very powerful lamp for his anti-poaching patrols. If this is shone on the river, particularly at the Junction Pool where there may be as many as 200 peal, the shoal moves away in a flurry, muddying the water by the disturbance, although they will settle after 20 minutes and again be catchable. Salmon, on the other hand, just stay in the light. Sometimes a torch has to be used to guide a large fish into the net then, half a dozen casts later, another peal may be hooked. Everyone agrees that voices in the dark do not disturb sea-trout, only other anglers. Vibration, such as clumsy wading, on the other hand, is to be avoided at all costs.

The Junction Pool is mainly fished by Hugh Dalgety, the riparian owner of the pool and 1 mile of the left bank of the river Mole, and John Snell of Newnham Barton, who farms the adjoining land. Hugh also rents the right bank of the Mole, opposite his own side, from the Wildfowl and Wetlands Trust. Additionally, he bought 1 mile of the right bank of the Taw from just above King's Nympton station to immediately above the Junction Pool.

After rain the Taw comes down much dirtier than the Mole, which clears quickly. Hugh says, 'The reason I bought the pool three years ago is because if it rains on Exmoor the Mole rises; if it rains on Dartmoor the Taw lifts. The only trouble is, there hasn't been a worthwhile rain for three years'.

The pool is 15 miles above the tide. Sea-liced fish reach the confluence within 24 hours of leaving salt water. Sea-trout start to arrive in numbers by the third week of May, and they are heavy fish. School peal appear with the July harvest moon. Hugh usually starts his night fishing with the first warm period in May, but does not stay out at night for more than two or three hours. He also catches peal on the fly by day when he is after salmon.

Having weak wrists, he had an 11-ft AFTM No 8 blank, in three pieces by Grey's of Alnwick, made up as a double-hander by Lance Nicholson of Dulverton. The line is usually a white double-

Dead River Pool on the Taw. Sea-trout lie under the trees.

tapered No 8 floater which is fished until about 1.00 am, after which he may change to a sink-tip. His reel is a Hardy No 8/9 Ultralite, and he uses Hardy knotless tapered leaders to 7 lb, or 6 lb when the school peal arrive and the water is low and clear.

His flies are usually Silver Stoat doubles or Waddingtons. The Loxy is a favourite, as is another local creation, the Piggins which is tied on an Esmond Drury treble of sizes varying from No 16 to No 10. The dressing is a silver body, a natural squirrel-tail wing and a few green hairs as throat hackle.

I asked Hugh to describe the catching of his best peal.

> On the second night after I had purchased the pool I was fishing quietly but, from the outer darkness, could hear a rustling in the waterside bushes. Poachers, I thought, a crocodile, or the ghost of an ancient angler. The hair rose on the back of my neck. The pool has often been poached, as it is close to the road. At that moment two things happened: I had a strong pull but the peal came off at the same moment that a powerful halogen beam illuminated me from across the river. It was Jeremy Boyd, the bailiff. I explained who I was, that I had purchased the pool, and that he'd caused me to loose my fish. 'Very sorry, Sir, I'll bugger off,' he said. Two nights later I had a savage take to a double Silver Stoat's Tail. That peal weighed 7 lb 4 oz and took out all my dressed line and some of the backing.

A guest of Hugh's in 1996 took a 9-lb peal out of Pump Pool just above the Junction Pool on the Taw. That fish ran 200 yd down to the railway bridge before surrendering.

The Teign, South Devon

On Dartmoor, 6 or 7 miles to the south-west of the moorland town of Chagford, the North Teign River is formed from small tributaries at 1,700 ft above sea level. Two miles to the west of Chagford it is joined by the South Teign. Since 1943 this small river has been substantially reduced, following the completion of the dam which created Fernworthy Reservoir, cutting off its feeder streams from the valley above the new construction. Some of the present small wild brown trout in the reservoir are the descendants of mixed brown and sea-trout, the spawning, many generations ago, of the peal which ran up the watercourse before the dam was closed. In 1949 and 1950, when I was fishing the reservoir, I caught some of these small silvery fishlets, which rarely exceeded ½ lb. In winter, water overflows the dam but, when the level in the reservoir drops below the lip of the dam in early summer, the South Teign relies on compensation water. The regulated flow is inadequate to allow the SouthTeign to retain its title of 'river'. It is now little more than a beautiful brook winding as it falls through a secret hidden valley.

From the junction of the two rivers, the Teign flows east and then south to emerge at Newton Abbot. Its length is about 35 miles. The main tributary is the River Bovey, which joins the Teign about 3 miles above the estuary.

The Teign is a spate river. Salmon fishing relies on rainfall both for catches and the entry of fish. Sea-trout enter the river and can be caught in low water. It has a heavy run of sea-trout, rod catches exceeding the salmon take by about five, six or even seven to one.

YEAR	Mar	April	May	June	July	Aug	Sept
1990	1	3	42	56	79	90	32
1991	1	4	42	40	120	114	85
1992	1	19	49	39	101	136	142
1993	8	9	36	52	210	230	239
1994	5	22	78	115	263	380	239

Monthly sea-trout rod catches on the Teign

In addition, a small number of sea-trout are taken each season without the month being recorded.

Roddy Rae's Bruce & Walker sea-trout fly rod with a built-on butt extension.

Roddy Rae of the Half Stone Sporting Agency is a fly-fishing instructor qualified by the Register of Fly-Fishing Instructors and Schools (REFFIS), and the Salmon & Trout Association National Instructor's Certificate (STANIC). Not only does he teach and let game fishing, but he also guides rods on many sections of the River Teign, of which he has intimate knowledge.

We met at Fingle Bridge, from where he took me 2 miles down the valley to his own left-bank salmon and sea-trout water which comprises 1½ miles of fishing above Upperton Weir.

The River Teign is hidden from view in many sections by steep hills on both sides. His section of the river is about 20 yd wide, heavily bushed, and roofed by trees. Roddy has cleared the bank in many places to allow access to the river, and cut spaces to allow room for the angler's back cast to extend. On my visit in July the beat was well populated by sea-trout, and I also saw a grilse. The peal were in the 1½–4-lb category, probably on their second and third spawning visits. There were almost no school peal on 22 July owing, I am sure, to persistent low water at the start of summer. At the time this lack of first-return peal, the schoolies, was also apparent on the rivers Dart and Lyd.

The river is not deep and has a rocky bed, and should only be fished at night in low water with a floating fly line. We also went to Drogo Pool, a long glide from stickles at the top to a salmon ladder at the tail; sea-trout run this ladder even in drought conditions. A spate would make the whole pool fishable for salmon, particularly above the falls, of which the fish ladder forms a part.

Drogo Pool is a wonderful sea-trout water, especially in the second half of the season – September in particular. It is also productive of salmon. An iron bridge crosses the pool towards the top; downstream of this bridge the river is narrowed by rocks jutting out from both banks, and above these rocks lie salmon and sea-trout –

a fruitful taking area. In low-water conditions peal move into the faster water towards the head of the pool to take advantage of the higher oxygen levels caused by the broken surface.

Roddy usually starts at the neck of the pool when he is night fishing in high summer, moves down to the middle and finishes above the weir. This progression provides sufficient fishing for one night.

Immediately above the falls, under the right bank, is a deep lie favoured by salmon, which used to house a water-powered generator to supply electricity to Castle Drogo. He not only fishes this place by casting downstream for salmon and peal but also by placing himself below the lip of the falls, casting his fly upstream for sea-trout at night. This upstream cast offers a different angle of presentation and requires a fast retrieve. Both speed and angle stimulate peal which may have

become used to rejecting flies cast down and across, followed by a slow retrieve.

The Upper Teign Fishing Association controls many miles of water between Steps Bridge and Chagford. The Lower Teign Fishing Association has charge of much of the lower river. Visitors' day tickets are available on both sections – see 'Finding Sea-trout Fishing' at the end of the book.

Fly only is the rule for both brown trout and sea-trout, although spinning is permitted for salmon, and worm for salmon after 1 June. The open rod seasons are: salmon, 1 February–30 September; sea-trout, 15 March–30 September.

In early April peal start to enter the lower sections of the river in the Chudleigh and Preston areas. By mid-April the first sea-trout appear at Upperton Pool, good-quality fish of 4 lb on average. A few peal of 5 and 6 lb are taken, but a double-figure sea-trout is a rarity on the upper

Roll-cast at night on the narrow, heavily treed river.

A 'doubled' fly line is threaded easily through the line guides
. . .

. . . and it is easier still if the rod is horizontal.

Drogo Pool on the River Teign holds many sea-trout and salmon.

Teign. Schoolies start to reach Upperton in July, and a few were visible on my visit on the 22nd of that month, rather late because of the low water and lack of a recent spate. There are no insurmountable obstructions to prevent fish reaching the top of the river, which they could achieve in two or three days.

Roddy has a rule on his water that anglers may not take more than six peal a night. Generally, he is not in favour of limits, which can lead anglers to try to reach the limit, instead of making conservation and enjoyment their priority. If an angler takes a salmon or two sea-trout he is usually a happy man, and will stop fishing and go home to show his wife. But if there is a limit he is more likely to continue. Angling also has a tradi-

tion of stories and memories of rare nights and days when all went right and many fish were taken. Provided one does not succumb to greed, these experiences are golden moments in an angler's life, which could not occur if the catch was restricted. So let preservation and conscience be the guide.

A sensible length of rod for the Teign is 9–10 ft, casting an AFTM No 7 floating line, as the river is mainly shallow. A sinking line could be used on Drogo Pool. Delicate presentation is essential because of the clear water. This leads Roddy to use a double-tapered AFTM No 6 light-coloured floating line in the early part of the season, but he may reduce to a No 5 line by the time school peal arrive.

Leaders are of floating, intermediate, or anti-skate braided nylon with a tippet of 3 or 4 ft of 4- 6- or 8-lb nylon. The diameter of the tippet is governed by the clarity of the water and the likely size of fish. In July and August he often goes down to 4 lb if he is fishing with a rod with a gentle action. He rarely degreases his tippet, as it is unnessary if he is using an intermediate braided leader. Nor does he grease the nylon when fishing a surface wake lure at night.

For sea-trout Roddy carries a 20-in diameter net with a metal ring, hinged at the top of the handle. Fish are carried in a net bag suspended at the back of his jacket, a camouflaged pigeon shooter's cover into which fish may be slid when he is wading.

He does not normally start fishing until he can no longer distinguish colours but can still see the far bank. When days are hot he will often start half an hour earlier when the air temperature starts to fall, as he has noticed that fish slash at sedges as the light fades; these peal he tempts with a Muddler stripped across the water surface. Such early starts allow a fish or two to be taken under a clear sky before the air becomes cold and peal 'go down'.

Roddy has not found any food inside the peal he has caught and cleaned, yet he has seen them rise to sedges at dusk. One evening, three years ago, he noticed a group of peal rising to a sedge hatch. Knotting on a White Moth he drifted it down over them and it was taken at once. Yet the next morning there was nothing in that fish's stomach. I sometimes wonder whether fish which appear to be feeding on surface flies at times are, in fact, just slashing at them.

Roddy is open-minded on methods of taking sea-trout on the fly following an experience on the Teifi. Waiting to fish as the light faded he watched a trout fisherman take three sewin schoolies on a dry Tup's Indispensible. After this he experimented with various methods, taking peal at night close to the riverbed on a Booby fished off an intermediate sinking line and Gold-head Nymphs and Montana Gold-heads off a floating fly line. The Booby, which was buoyant because of the foam or polystyrene head, remained clear of the riverbed, but was kept down by the sinking fly line. Gold-heads also account for school peal when cast upstream in rough, fast water by day. The upstream Gold-head has also worked for him by day on the rivers Taw and Spey.

Most of his night flies are dressed on Slipstream aluminium tubes of ½–1½ in, depending on the month and the freshness of the fish. The longer flies are used early in the season, reducing, even to a ¼-in plastic tube, in high summer and low, clear water. The longer a fish has been in the water, the smaller the fly required to take him. He favours Partridge type X3 needle-eyed black outpoint trebles in sizes No 10 and No 12, kept in line with the tube body by a silicone sleeve, and he has three favourite fly patterns: the Silver Stoat's Tail with a silver Mylar body ribbed at the tail, a sparse wing of squirrel tail dyed black, and jungle cock eyes; the Alexandra, with a Mylar silver body, ribbed oval silver tinsel, and a peacock sword wing; and the Dunkeld of standard dressing as in John Veniard's *Fly Dressing Guides*. The Dunkeld is particularly attractive to fish in peaty-coloured water after rain.

He has devised a fly for clear moonlit nights which he is reluctant to claim as his own, commenting that most flies are variations on established themes. It is the Teign Ghost, a bright-coloured fly on a silver-Mylar-bodied aluminium Slipstream tube, with a pearl metal flash wing, two strips of duck wing dyed red, and jungle cock eyes. He is sure that a light colour is best for a moonlit night, and a black fly on dark nights. He does not use Beta lights or luminous strip. He does not favour droppers on a small river such as the Teign, but he will use a large fly as a dropper on a wide river.

On his narrow water one needs to start fishing whilst kneeling and keeping back from the edge of the bank, and cast a short line. The casting distance can be gradually increased, but it is a mistake to begin by casting a long line, as one covers and frightens the fish with the line before they have had a chance to see the fly.

Roddy has had considerable success on the River Spey whilst trotting Gold-head nymphs down the water by day. He holds the rod high whilst the weight of the metal gold bead head sinks the nymph down to fish resting close to the the river bed, which it searches as it carried along by the current. He intends to try this method on the Teign.

He is also experimenting with the use of 15-ft leaders tapered to a 2-lb point to fish a weighted nymph by day. Such fine nylon would be liable to snap when a fish takes, were it not for the addition of a short 4-lb strip of elastic Optima High Power Gum between the line and the leader. Having seen an angler take a sea-trout by day on a green caterpillar imitation, he is sure there is wide scope for new daylight methods.

Sea-trout cast a spell on him at the early age of ten years. A sea-trout of just over 3 lb from the River Leven, which runs out of Loch Lomond, took his wriggling worm when he was after brown trout. He will never forget that first awe-inspiring battle. Since then he has been fascinated. They are the only game fish in our waters which he considers to be truly elusive and unpredictable. He knows when brown trout are likely to feed, and can predict when salmon will take and where they will lie, according to the water conditions. But sea-trout? One never knows what to expect.

His best sea-trout weighed 7½ lb, and came from Ashton Pool on the water of the Lower Teign Fishing Association. Taken in May 1990, it was part of a remarkable bag which included peal of 6½, 6 and 5 lb, all taken on a Silver Stoat. They were caught by casting across the lip of the weir at Ashton before it was altered and renewed. Despite his thoughtful dedication to the pursuit of peal, I doubt if he will take a better bag.

The Dovey, West Wales

The Dovey rises nearly 3,000 ft above the sea in Llyn Craiglyn to the north-west of Pennant. It falls steeply to Cemmaes, then more steadily, whilst becoming wider, past Machynlleth to the tidal reaches and the sea at Aberdovey. The total distance is in the region of 32 miles.

It is a beautiful river: hills reach up on many sides, some 2,000 ft towards the sky, the trees are many and varied, the river depths range from shallow and deep, there are open and secluded pools, and large and small sewin (the Welsh name for sea-trout) abound.

There are many tributaries to provide prolific spawning areas for salmon and sea-trout, but these streams tend to dry out in times of drought, resulting in the death of young fish. The establishment of a migratory fish hatchery is offsetting the adverse effects of increased afforestation, drainage and low rainfall. In common with other rivers in England and Wales, afforestation and extra drainage have resulted in short-lived floods increasing the spate characteristics of the Dovey. As with the Towy, this means a reduced salmon-fishing period after each spate, but sea-trout are more reliable, and are caught on fly in low water as well as during the run-off of a spate.

The Dovey is one of the best sea-trout rivers in Wales, although it does not quite match the rod take of the Towy and the Teifi. Its sewin are large; many anglers take a fish of 8 or 9 lb during the season, whilst 2–5 lb is common.

Early-season heavy sewin are occasionally taken by rod in late April as high as Pen-y-Bont Falls on the Brigands Inn water at Mallwyd, and both they and salmon may carry sea-lice. There are no major obstructions on the river which fish are unable to jump, even in the cold water of spring, between the tide and Pen-y-Bont.

Sewin in the 2–5-lb category increase in the river in late June and throughout July. Whitling, also called schoolies and shoalies, which can weigh up to 1 lb, enter in late July, increasing their numbers in August. Throughout the mid-season and early autumn large sea-trout continue to enter the river.

There are catch limits to rods of three sewin a day, and shoalies of less than 12 in must be returned to the river. There is also a daily limit of two salmon or grilse. The open rod season for both salmon and sea-trout is from 20 March to 17 October. Natural bait fishing is not allowed before 15 April or after 7 October. The open season is subject to additional regulations on the major length of the river controlled by the New Dovey Fishery Association (1929) Ltd, which issues limited tickets to visitors. The addresses of ticket distributors are given under 'Finding Sea-trout fishing' at the end of this book. No visitors' tickets are issued after the last Saturday in August.

The association has a rule that only fly-fishing is allowed unless the river is high and coloured. In that case the Head Keeper of the association puts out yellow flags at prominent places, and one can then worm and spin on the 20 miles of the Association's waters.

At Mallwyd, upstream of the New Dovey sections, is the Brigands Inn, where I was entertained by John and Julia Garside. The Brigands is a fishing hotel of note, and John is a skilled sewin angler able to give expert advice to those fishing the 2½ miles of the hotel's waters on the Dovey and the Cleifion.

Monthly sewin catches on the Dovey and tributaries over recent seasons have been as the table below shows:

A fly-fishing rod for this river should be in the region of 10 ft 6 in, capable of dealing with large sea-trout and the occasional salmon or grilse. If it is of medium action, it should be matched by an AFTM No 7 or 8 floating fly line on a reel of not less than 3⅝ in diameter. Spare spools should be available loaded with sink-tips for the deeper pools and faster flows. These sink-tips may be slow, medium or fast sinking. Cheap tapered sinking lines are often bought by those living in the area and 3 or 4 ft or more of the tip cut off. This is then joined to the end of a floating fly line of good quality by a braided sleeve junction. Two inches each of the floating and sink-tip lines are inserted and superglued into the ends of the braided sleeve, the surface of which is then varnished and smoothed over with plastic.

Few anglers bother with tapered leaders; they use nylon of about 8 or 10 lb straight off the spool, or a minimum of 6 lb in very clear water. If one is fishing a large tube of 2 or 2½ in on the point at night nylon of 12 lb should be used.

A well-designed point tube would incorporate a black body ribbed with silver tinsel, a wing of squirrel dyed black, orange hackle and two jungle cock cheeks. This creates a local fly known as the Dovey Black & Orange.

Tail: Red swan
Rib: Silver tinsel
Body: Black floss silk
Hackle: Orange hen
Wing: Squirrel dyed black
Cheeks: Jungle cock
Head: Black varnish
Hook: No 4, 6 and 8 double or 1-in plastic tube

	April	May	June	July	Aug	Sept	Oct	FISH RELEASED
1992	0	5	77	95	176	32	8	not available
1993	2	12	201	482	374	230	30	247
1994	1	22	266	532	648	360	48	832

Sewin, whose month of capture are not recorded, have not been included.

with No 10 Partridge type X1 outpoint treble in black

As a dropper or point fly, the Haslam salmon fly is also popular.

Tag: Flat silver tinsel
Butt: White floss silk
Tail: Small golden pheasant crest
Body: Flat silver tinsel
Rib: Oval silver tinsel
Throat hackle: Blue jay, or guinea fowl dyed blue
Wing: Hen pheasant tail, tied slim
Horns: Blue/yellow macaw tied in so that they curve along the sides of the wings with the tips crossing over each other above the tail

Head: Black varnish
Hook: No 4, 6, 8 or 10, single or double

The Black Pennell on a single No 6 or No 8 hook or dressed on a 1-in plastic tube is also popular. Another favoured pattern is the Stoat's Tail, preferably with the addition of jungle cock cheeks.

There is one method of daytime fly-fishing for small sea-trout up to about 2 lb which is effective on the Dovey. A team of two or three small flies is cast upstream over a shoal of sewin and then stripped back fast. A floating line should be used. But it only works when an upstream wind roughens the surface of the river; in calm conditions it is a waste of time.

There is free fishing on a stretch upstream of this bridge on the Dovey above Mallwyd.

Pen-y-Bont Pool on the Brigand's Inn water at Mallwyd is suited to the worm and spinning.

Many anglers carry a net, but on major stretches of the river sewin may be beached on shingle banks.

The best nights for the fly are as a spate drops away; good fishing continues in the settled conditions which may follow.

As I have said, natural baits are not allowed anywhere on the Dovey before 15 April or after 7 October. At other times they are allowed on the water of the Brigands Inn, but not on the New Dovey sections unless the yellow flags fly in high and coloured water.

The brandling is the best worm for sea-trout, and can be used in both warm and cold water. It is usually found in manure heaps and piles of old grass cuttings. To fish the worm close to the riverbed some additional weight is needed. This is often provided by a pierced bullet on the reel line above the swivel at the top of the trace.

Two or three brandlings should be baited onto a single hook of size No 8 or No 10, but it is wise to rub one's hands in earth first to disguise any human taint. Salmon need a larger hook of size No 2 or No 4, and three good-sized blue-headed lobworms. When a sewin takes the worm the response strike should be quick, unlike the delayed strike for salmon. Of course, not all takes will be either salmon or sewin; there are eels in the river, and also flounders.

The most useful outfit for both spinning and worming is a long rod – 10 ft is suitable – and a fixed-spool reel. Some anglers fish with a fly rod and centre-pin reel filled with monofilament for the worm, but this cannot be used as a spinning rod.

As salmon will take the worm as well as sea-trout, one ought not to fish very fine nylon. A reel line of 12 lb with a 10-lb trace would be the minimum needed.

The Toby is the favourite artificial bait on the river for salmon, whilst a No 2 Mepp Aglia cast upstream, or up and across, does very well for sewin.

The Towy, South Wales

In its source reaches in the Cambrian Mountains the Towy forms the county boundary between Powys to the east and Dyfed to the west. Initially, the river runs due south to Llandovery, then south-west to Llangadog and Llandeilo, where it turns west to Carmarthen and the estuary in Carmarthen Bay.

Much of the fishing in the river is controlled by angling associations with waiting lists for full membership, but they issue day and week tickets to visitors, both through hospitality and as an aid to tourism. An excellent 12-mile section of the lower river between Landeilo and Nantgaredig is mainly managed or owned by Hamdden Ltd, a subsidiary of Welsh Water, which lets fishing by the day, week and season. Fishing continues down to the tidal reaches near Carmarthen. The controlling organization is listed under 'Finding Sea-trout Fishing' at the end of the book. Upstream of Llandovery sea-trout fishing continues to Nant-y-Bai and beyond.

The Towy produces a greater number of sea-trout per season than any other river in England and Wales according to the Environment Agency Fisheries Statistics. Not only are many of the fish of notable size, but the average weight is high. In 1993 close to 3,000 sewin were taken by rods, and this rose to nearly 5,000 in 1994. The salmon rod catch in these years was also substantial – 388 and 896 respectively.

On my visit, I met Gareth Edwards, the Chairman of Hamdden Ltd, Max James, the retired Towy Head Keeper and Cyril Fox, the Head Keeper at Abercothi at the Golden Grove and Abercothi Fisheries between Llandeilo and Nantgaredig. The water level was ideal for night sea-trout fishing at 2.9 ft on the Abercothi gauge. The lowest level is in the region of 2.4 ft, and it is sustained at this level by compension water from Llyn Brianne Reservoir situated a few miles below the source of the river. For salmon the best height is between 3 and 4 ft on the gauge, which is 7 miles above the sea, but they are caught even when the gauge is as high as 6 ft, provided the level is falling, and as low as 2.5 ft. But when the river is high sea-trout and salmon tend to run through the fishery on their way upstream.

Heavy spates colour the water considerably but do not last long. Max commented that years before a full spate might not reduce to a fishable clarity for three days, and then there would be five days' fishing before the water had gone. As a boy Gareth was also told to wait until the third day. In those years, in high water, sea-trout carrying sea-lice could be caught at Llandeilo as the high level was maintained for long enough for them to run 20 miles upriver in 48 hours, before the sea-lice dropped from their flanks. To catch salmon now, one must be out the morning after the spate peak, and the water is only fishable over the next two days. Both migratory fish run in low water, but salmon only at night. Max has heard and seen salmon moving upstream at 3.00 am in the lowest possible water.

The Towy is a substantial river, with attractive tree-lined banks in many places – attractive, that is, to sewin which favour rivers overhung with trees and other growth. There are also troughs in the bedrock under the trees, much favoured as lies by heavy sewin. Elsewhere, as in other rivers, the tails of the pools provide the best lies.

Spring tides in the estuary, 7 miles below the Abercothi Fishery, do not have a noticeable effect on catches, and the full moon does not make for good fishing; the darkest nights are the best. All three of the people I spoke to await full darkness before fishing steady lies, but will fish rough water runs in the half-light.

There are otters on the river. They feed mainly on eels, but will steal an angler's fish if it is left unattended on the bank. In their journeys up and down the river they do not disturb sewin to the extent of making them uncatchable, provided they swim straight through the pool – if they hunt a pool it is a different matter!

Goosanders are far too common, and eat many salmon and sea-trout parr, and cormorants are also greedy predators. Licences have to be obtained to shoot cormorants but, as one enter-prising keeper told me on another river, 'They're protected, Charles, but only beyond a distance of 50 yd'. Another keeper ran a metal detector over the ground below a cormorant roosting tree beside his river and recovered nearly 100 salmon micro-tags, which had been placed in the fore-heads of migrating smolts by the Environment Agency, from the droppings of the birds.

There has been some reduction in migratory fish populations, due partly to increased rod pres-sure, but also to modern farming methods, increased land drainage and afforestation. The acidity of the river, which increased as a result of tree planting, is now being reduced by the addi-tion of lime to Llyn Brianne Reservoir. Evidence

Guardians of sea-trout at risk from mink.

of a higher pH was apparent in the establishment of ranunculus weedbeds, which I saw in the water.

The estuary net season for salmon and sea-trout opens on 1 March and closes on 31 August; the rod season is from 26 January to 17 October for salmon and 18 March to 17 October for sea-trout. The nets thus open before the sewin rods. Even so, the Abercothi Fishery yields heavy sea-trout right from the start of the season – sewin of 5 lb and above are common, and fish in double figures are not unusual. Not many fish reach the higher sections of the river until late May. Heavy sewin continue to enter until June when the average size starts to reduce, but 3- and 4-lb sea-trout are still common. June also marks the start of the return of those smolts which went to sea earlier that year. Some Towy smolts go to sea early in February, returning in May. Cyril and Max refered to first-return sea-trout as schoolies or shoalies, the equivalent of the Devon school peal and the Scottish finnock.

Gareth keeps a fishing diary, and looking back over the years he notes that it is from the first week in June that the majority of sewin are caught at Abercothi. He has taken sea-trout in April and May, when the fish are large and sea-liced, but the period from June onwards provide the cream. Max considers that May, June and July are the finest months. A mixture of shoalies and second- and third-return sewin, together with a scattering of heavy fish, continue to enter throughout the summer, with a marked increase in large specimens in the autumn.

There is no rule that shoalies must be returned to the water, but with a reduction in runs of fish in recent years this is now a widely accepted practice at Abercothi and among the angling associations. There is also a daily catch limit of four migratory fish; if one has caught one salmon and three sea-trout, or any other combination, one must leave the river.

Night fishing is by fly, usually with rods of 9 ft 6 in to 10 ft 6 in, which are capable of handling both the large sewin for which the river is renowned and salmon. What surprised me is that most fishing is done at night with sinking fly lines. This is no doubt because of the considerable depth of the river and the speed and volume of flow in many areas.

Max uses an AFTM No 8 double-tapered or weight-forward sink-tip line as well as a slow sinker and even a WetCel 2. As he said: 'I like to feel the water drag on the line as it swings across. I know where my fly is searching, and feel the slightest touch to the fly as the line is between my fingers.' If he feels the maddening plucks and pulls that are so common when rain is due, he does a figure-of-eight turn, strikes, and the fish is usually his!

Max went up the river to fish one night and caught eight sewin between 5 and 9 lb. He took the fish to the owner of the water the next morning, and the owner asked him to telephone a friend who was going to fish the next night and tell him where he had caught the fish. The following morning the friend phoned back to say that he had had a wonderful night, taking five fish between 3½ and 4½ lb. 'You must have been using a floating line, Bill' said Max. 'What a disappointment. You should have used a sinking line to go down to the heavy fish.'

By day, with the gauge on about 2.9 ft, in fast ripply water, Cyril fishes small traditional wet flies in sizes No 10 and No 12, single hook: Mallard & Claret, Peter Ross and Teal & Silver Blue. If the water is higher, and thus more coloured, he uses a Teal & Silver Blue in a larger size, perhaps No 8. He also uses these flies in fast water at dusk whilst waiting for the night. When it is fully dark he changes to tube flies and Waddingtons. Max commented: 'A live sparrow, that's what he'd like.'

Gareth fishes a floating fly line in fast water at dusk on warm evenings; fish move more freely to the lure at that time if they are fished just beneath the surface. He changes to a sinking line in full darkness.

The tube flies and Waddingtons are between

1 and 2 in long, although sometimes even a 3-in tube is used. Most flies used on the Towy are considerably larger than those used on other rivers.

Max dresses many flies for anglers, and all three agreed on the general methods of construction. The hook used most frequently is a black Partridge X1 round-eye No 8 outpoint treble, with an aluminium tube without any added weight. Sometimes on dark nights and when the water is coloured a Beta light is fitted to the shank of the treble hook, held there by a clear plastic tube. This glow is permanent and does not have to be recharged with a torch.

Most anglers like the treble to be held in line with the fly body by a rubber tube like a bicycle valve. Max dresses flies with the rubber tube for other anglers, but for himself prefers to knot the treble to the nylon leader without a rubber sleeve. Without a sleeve, shoalies, which he does not want to catch and then have to release, are not hooked securely. They tend to fall off, whilst heavy sewin, perhaps because of their larger mouths, engulf the whole fly and are securely hooked, whether or not it has a sleeve. With Waddingtons a rubber sleeve can be used to keep the treble in line or, on 2-in shanks, one or two strands of 30-lb nylon whipped to both Partridge Waddington and treble shanks has the same effect.

In general, both tubes and Waddingtons are dressed with black bodies ribbed with oval silver tinsel. The wing may be of peacock herl and bronze turkey with a throat hackle of blue cock fibres.

Gareth sometimes uses a dropper at dusk in fast water, but although some anglers use them in the dark, he does not. At any time on the Towy, which is a river of large sewin, there is the chance of hooking the fish of a lifetime. When playing such a prize it is unwise to have a second fly trailing free to catch in snags or be taken by a second fish.

Max has developed his own special fly. 'I can honestly say that it has caught over 1,000 fish,' he says. The body is made of the long shank of a streamer hook, which is cut at the bend after the dressing is complete. Strong nylon is turned around the back of a No 8 treble and whipped onto the shank of the treble. A gap of about ¼ in is allowed between the eye of the treble and the cut-off end of the streamer shank. The two nylon ends are bound to the shank after being roughened by a cigarette lighter. The bodies of both the treble and the streamer shank are of flat silver tinsel, ribbed with oval silver tinsel. Cock hackles, dyed blue, are tied in at the neck and butt of the streamer shank and just behind the treble eye. The wing is 2 in long of peacock herl and bronze turkey, and there are two jungle cock eyes one third of the length of the shank of the streamer hook. I estimated the overall length of the fly he showed me to be in the region of 2½ or 3 in.

His leaders are not tapered, just plain Maxima Chameleon or a German nylon called Strong (not Stren), which Max prefers. They are usually 9 ft long, but may be reduced to 6 ft on a sinking fly line in coloured water. 'Now then,' said Max, 'do you want to know the breaking strain? Personally, I never use less than 15 lb. At the moment I am using 18½ lb.'

'What, then, is the size of your net?' I asked.

'I never use one. I can tail or beach the fish. If I lose one, I can cope with that. The chances are I'll catch another.'

Gareth always carries a net for sea-trout, but beaches them if possible.

Max uses such a heavy nylon leader to give a good turnover of a large tube or Waddington to extend it under the far bank. The fly then starts to fish at once. If 8-lb nylon is used the fly turns back on the leader in the air when it is cast and fails to reach the far water. By the time the line has been curved by the current and thus straightened the leader, the fly is only fishing half or two thirds of the river. If a cast is made with an 18-lb leader and, as soon as the fly hits the water and starts to sink a single upstream mend is made, the fly fishes the whole width of the river. Even those areas 4 or 6 ft deep under the far bank can be fished effectively if one wades out from the shallow side.

Gareth couples a weight-forward or double-tapered line rated AFTM No 8 floater, sink-tip or intermediate sinkier to a leader of 8 or 10 lb of Maxima Chameleon. His choice of strength depends on the size of fly and the clarity of the water. Cyril also uses the same nylon. Their leaders have a blood bight loop tied at the end, which is attached, loop to loop, to a superglued braided loop on the end of the fly line.

In early May, four or five years ago, Gareth fished Abercothi Pool which is not normally one of the best. It was a humid night, overcast, sweaty, and with light rain – almost a mid-July night, good for sea-trout. A run of fresh, heavily sea-liced sewin came in and he landed five or six of up to 8 lb and all over 5 lb. In that season he was unable to fish frequently because of other engagements, but nevertheless by the end of the season he had taken about 20 sea-trout averaging just over 5 lb.

All three of my informants found that heavy rain made for poor results at night, but a warm drizzle was likely to be good. They also agreed that sewin are liable to pluck and pull at the fly without being hooked when rain is due in a few hours. They recalled that about six years before, salmon and sea-trout were being trapped to introduce radio tags into their stomachs. There were 77 sewin in the trap, of which 23 were in double figures and one weighed 21 lb.

Very large sewin are rarely caught on a fly. They move little, rest under rocky ledges in the same pool for long periods, and sometimes go back to the estuary. Even so, the river yields a few 14- and 15-pounders each season to rods.

It is clear that sewin move from daytime lies in midriver and deep lies under the banks to the heads and tails of pools at dusk. They also move into shallower areas. Gareth pointed out a deep place under the far bank. 'The water is slow there and not often fished, but there are heavy fish there. Their noise occasionally would be enough to frighten anybody. It is not fisherman's tales: they're like cows wallowing, real big boys – pigs, we call them.'

It was agreed that when the water is low and warm sewin tend to go into quiet, deep, almost currentless places where the depth provides coolness. These positions also make low demands on energy expenditure. They are also favoured by poachers with nets, who come from Abergavenny, and from Hereford and Ross-on-Wye if the river Wye is fishing badly.

Cyril considers that one should wait until the far bank cannot be seen before starting to fish at night. This is because fish tend to move from pool to pool at dusk, and from lie to lie in a pool. They must settle before one starts fly-fishing.

All three agreed on the question of lights and disturbance. Max said: 'If I was fishing with Gareth and he hooked a double figure fish I would use a torch to land it. A bird in the hand is worth two in the bush. You could then go in again and hook a fish, even if the torch had shone on the water.' This coincides with the view of a friend of mine who fishes close to a busy road; car lights sweep across the water, but he still catches peal.

Cyril agreed. 'I was ghillying one night for a man and, whilst landing a fish for him I shone my torch on the water. "It's like Blackpool," he said. "No," I replied. "You go in again." First cast he had another fish.' Nevertheless, it is clearly not sensible to be careless in the use of a torch, so keep lights to a minimum.

Max confirmed that sound makes no difference. 'When Cyril and I are fishing we are always talking. You could hear us in Carmarthen.' 'What I think makes a difference is movement,' Gareth added. 'Keep still and don't stumble about.'

In high water both worm and artificial spinning baits are used by day, but upstream flies are seldom used in low water. Cyril likes to put three lobworms on a sliced hook for salmon. For sea-trout he uses brandlings on a No 16 hook. The brandlings are fished from a long, flexible rod to reach over the river, and with a small weight. The flexibility of the rod tip is his indicator of a take, as it bends to the slightest tweak. A gentle rod tip is also necessary to absorb shocks to his reel line and trace, both of which are 4-lb monofilament fished off a fixed-spool reel.

He collects his brandlings from manure heaps. The lobworms are brought to the surface of his lawn by a novel method which I christened the 'Fox Electric Fork'. An electric cable is clipped to the metal of the prongs of a garden fork, then plugged into a socket in his house. Having plunged the fork into the lawn he goes into the house, turns on the current and watches out of a window. After about ten minutes he switches off the current, goes out and collects the worms. By shifting the fork three or four times, he is able to collect enough worms for his needs. Some of his friends do not switch off the current, but collect the worms whilst wearing gumboots, but this can be dangerous when the grass is wet. Hungry birds, spotting the feast, come down but do not stay long: 'When they feel a tickle to their feet they soon hop off, and so do any stray cats.'

In high water, when the Abercothi gauge is at 3 or 4 ft, the Flying C is used for spinning; its weight causes it to fish deep in the water. It accounts for both salmon and sea-trout, as there is no control over which is caught.

In low water Gareth spins on 8-lb nylon for both fish with a little bait, a No 1 Mepp Longue or a small Quill Minnow. Cyril prefers an Irish Lane Minnow.

Before Cyril's time at Abercothi there was a keeper called Ken Edwards. He caught as many fish as anyone by using 18-lb nylon and a No 4 Mepp Aglia, and he never changed from March until the end of the season.

It is said that a sea-trout is a migratory brown trout. Simon Steel, Senior Fisheries Technician of the Environment Agency, South West, told me that in his juvenile electro-surveys he is unable to distinguish between brown-trout and sea-trout fry. In a letter to me dated 4 July 1996 he said: 'The site at Higher Cherrybrook Bridge [on Dartmoor], which we surveyed that afternoon, yielded 167 trout fry, which I expect may have been the progeny of sea-trout spawning.'

Max agreed. When he walked the Towy tributaries to observe spawning, the first thing he noticed were several brown-trout redds. Just upstream there might be a spawning pair of sewin of 6 or 7 lb each. The brown trout would try to slip beneath the hen sewin to eat the eggs as they were extruded from her vent. The cock sewin would drive the brown trout away, but if a cock sea-trout was not present, cock brown trout and parr would fertilize the eggs.

Shad arrive in the Towy in June, and Max had a novel idea for cooking them. 'They are very bony. The best way to cook a shad is to wet some newspaper, put the shad in it, put it in the oven and roast it. When it is cooked, throw the shad away and eat the newspaper. I knew a novice rod who caught a shad and, thinking it was a sea-trout, gave it to his best friend. He choked on the bones.'

The Fowey, Cornwall

There are three major sea-trout rivers in Cornwall, the Camel, the Fowey and the Lynher. All rise on Bodmin Moor but flow in different directions. The Camel runs south-east for several miles, then west to Wadebridge and the sea at Padstow. The Fowey rises to the east of the hill called Brown Willy, 1,400 ft above the sea on High Moor, and initially flows south-east past Sibblyback Reservoir (from which it receives compensation water) and Golitha Falls. It then turns west towards Bodmin before flowing south through Lostwithiel to the sea at Fowey. The Lynher rises near Trewint, just south of Altarnun to the north of East Moor. It then runs south-east through Rilla Mill and under Newbridge near

Callington to join the Tamar estuary south of Saltash.

They all have some common features, the most notable being a proliferation of bankside trees which restrict fly-fishing opportunities, particularly at night. Anglers thus tend to rely on spinning and fishing natural baits for salmon, as well as fly at night for peal where a clear space allows. Whilst the use of natural baits is common, they are not allowed on some sections.

Major lengths of the rivers are controlled by associations and clubs, which are usually full with waiting lists. Day tickets are widely available but, in general, not after 30 September. This is no restriction for visiting peal anglers because the sea-trout rod season ends then on all three rivers. It does restrict salmon fishing by non-members, as the main runs are in November and December; the open seasons continue until late in the year: 15 December on the Camel and the Fowey, and 14 October on the Lynher.

All three rivers can be classified as spate waterways, with rapid rises and falls in water levels after several hours of rain. Usually, the first spate after a long drought will come down heavily discoloured, but subsequent rises are clearer if they occur at short intervals. The fishing period as the water drops back is short, perhaps only two days unless rain continues to fall.

Runs of sea-trout occur at much the same time as on other West Country peal rivers. Large peal start to arrive in May, reducing in size as the season progresses. School peal enter in July and August, and at any time a heavy fish may appear. The Fowey has been the most prolific sea-trout river in Cornwall for many years. Reported catches are:

	Fowey	Camel	Lynher
1992	970	370	390
1993	896	861	302
1994	1118	1332	347
	2984	2563	1039

Given to The National Trust in 1953 by Viscount Clifden, the Lanhydrock Estate includes a double-bank section of the Fowey from the bridge below Bodmin Parkway station to the Restormel waterworks, a distance of approximately 2 miles. Being only 4 miles above the tide, it regularly has sea-liced fish.

The Lanhydrock Angling Association has a membership of 70 and there is a waiting list. This need not deter the visitor or local non-member who wishes to fish for peal, as six day tickets are available each day from Monday to Friday from 1 April to 30 September, although not after that during the main salmon run. Tickets are issued at the Estate Office, which is open from 9.00 am to 5.00 pm from Monday to Friday, and it is unusual for all tickets to be taken. A weekly licence is also available at a very reasonable price. All anglers must produce an Environment Agency rod licence at the time of buying their Lanhydrock permit. The Association does not allow the use of natural baits.

Ralph Hands a member of the Association, has been fishing for 72 years since, if his memory is correct, he started at the age of eight. Many anglers follow long-established proven methods: spinning, flies, worms. They do what others do, as witness the fashion among many anglers for a certain pattern of fly after a night of notable success with it by a garrulous angler. The following year a different lure holds sway. This is not Ralph's way. His path is his alone.

At the age of eight, without a rod but equipped with a length of string, a few inches of gut and a grasshopper, he caught trout. Not having a rod to sneak out through the trees, he had to conceal himself some other way. He used the water – the rough place at the pool run-in where ripples hid his outline. Drifted down upon the disturbed surface to the extremity of the string the grasshopper swung to one side then struggled towards the bank and the calm water on one side of the main flow. Then came the flash of a turning flank and the longed-for bathplug gurgle as the hopper was sucked from sight. His approach is just as experimental today – he has a combined salmon and sea-trout lure called the Horror.

Ralph has no argument with the use of natural baits, but would like to see a ban on ledgering. Many ledger weights become snagged, the line breaks, the worm remains anchored, swaying in the current, and a fish sucks it down. It is unlikely to break free and may die.

A naturalist by inclination, his enemy is the mink, killer of much that moves along the river bank, swims in the water and skims above the ripples. Today there are no moorhens at Lanhydrock, and the nest of the only recently observed water rail was raided and destroyed. He found two dead otter kits and suspects the same dark, sinuous culprit.

There are brighter apects to Lanhydrock. There are kingfishers and dippers, and the otter is returning. In 1995 Ralph found four chewed salmon on the bank and took them home for his neighbour's cat; an otter was the likely culprit. He has seen a bird he recognized as a goshawk, and then there was an episode with a heron and an eel. Seated on a log beside the river near Respryn Bridge in winter, he saw a heron emerge from a ditch. In its beak there squirmed an eel. The heron stalked across the grass to a substantial wooden fence, slapped the eel hard against it, then gulped it down, all 2 ft of it. 'You could see the undulations as it slid down to be absorbed in the heron's maw.'

When he goes out to catch a migratory fish, Ralph has in mind a combined operation for both salmon and sea-trout if he is fishing in coloured spate water by day. He casts his large, weighted tube fly, the Horror, off a fixed-spool reel filled with 14-lb monofilament. The tube is retrieved fast and is thus taken at speed by fish which have no time to inspect the breaking strain of the nylon. The tube does not revolve, it swims arrow-like through the water, forcing a fish to take its chance or miss it. He has no time for spinning minnows – 'Whoever saw a live minnow going round and round in a river.'

Ralph Hands's Horror sea-trout and salmon fly.

The problem is to make the Horror fish at a depth of 1 or 2 ft beneath the surface. To this end, in addition to some added weight, he has two ½-in feather butts, stiffened with varnish, at the head of the tube and pointing down, rather like the vane of a plug bait. The plastic tube is about 2 in in length and dressed with whole guinea-fowl feathers along the flank. The ringed eye of a treble (No 8 by day or No 10 at night for a short peal tube of 1 or 1½ in) is slightly flattened so that it can be pulled into the tail of the tube. Golden-barred cock pheasant breast feathers replace guinea fowl in the autumn as the leaves on the trees change colour and so does the water.

At night he fishes with a 9-ft rod, a dark floating line to match the colour of the water, and small Horror or black fly. He notes that peal swim close to the riverbed and look up towards the sky, against which a black lure is clearly seen in silhouette. The leader is untapered 14-lb nylon.

Ralph uses another unusual lure for peal: the Red Gill black rubber elver which he buys from the tackle shop. The nylon leader is threaded through the elver in the manner of a tube fly and knotted to a treble hook, the eye of which is thrust into the vent of the elver. 'In spring shoals of elvers come in to the river', he says. 'I have seen them eaten by peal.'

At the age of 80 with a groggy knee and a replacement hip, Ralph needs a wading staff, and also a tailer and a net, all of which he manages to carry. The collapsible arms of the Y-shaped net are enclosed in a cloth sheath suspended across his shoulder on a leather strap, resembling the arrow quiver of a longbow archer. The wading staff and tailer are combined, the tailer being attached to the top of the wading staff with the wire noose enclosed in another canvas sheath. The tailer can be erected and held in position at the top of the staff by a finger-tightened knurled nut when the time comes to land a fish.

Night fishing commences with a fly. 'But if I see a big fish moving I put a Horror over him from my fixed-spool reel and spinning rod.' Ralph rarely

Ralph Hands's combined wading staff and tailer.

wades; he prefers to find a place where he can fish from the bank or off a spit of gravel.

He studies fish lies with care and finds them where an underwater obstruction creates a 'V' in the flow. He often takes fish in the 'V' either in front of or behind the obstruction. He also finds fish in the necks of pools, where they pause on their upstream journey, and in the wide tails in a full flow. His best peal of 9½ lb came in May 1994 from a 'V' caused by a boulder in the tail of a pool where it had paused to rest after working up a long line of rapids. It took about ten minutes to subdue and was netted, although most of his night peal are beached.

Asked to describe the best night conditions, he cited high humidity and cloud cover. If fish are caught 12 hours after a spring tide they would be sea-liced and, in May or June, heavy!

Ralph has a fund of fishing stories, of which the following is one.

> I was fishing one day with Dick Jones, who hooked a heavy fish which was hard to control. Round and round the pool it went. Dick shouted, 'You'll have to help me land it.' As I reached forward, he shouted, 'I've lost my hat.'
>
> 'Bugger the hat,' I responded, 'let's land the fish.'
>
> I grabbed the tail as the salmon drifted in under the overhang whilst I was flat on my stomach. I felt an awful pain in my hand. I couldn't hold the fish, and it escaped, leaving the treble in the flesh of my thumb. I had to have the hook taken out and the thumb stitched. Later, when we met George Henwood, the bailiff, we told him that if he saw a ragged-arsed salmon wearing a hat, it was ours.

The Hampshire Avon

The Avon is formed in the Vale of Pewsey from two streams the East Avon and West Avon, which join at Scales Bridge at Rushall. The river then runs by or through Upavon, East Chisenbury,

Fittleton, Netheravon, Figheldean, Durrington and Bulford to Amesbury. This section of the river provides good trout and grayling fishing, but just as good, if not better, is the section from Amesbury to Salisbury, which passes through the Woodford Valley. Above Salisbury, it is joined by the Nadder which has itself been added to by the Wylye at Quidhampton.

The Avon is augmented just below Salisbury by the Bourne, and the Ebble comes in 2½ miles downstream of the town centre at Bodenham. Between Salisbury and Christchurch the river, now much enlarged, changes in character. It is no longer a trout stream; fishing is predominantly for salmon and coarse fish. The best of the salmon fishing is between Fordingbridge and Christchurch, the most seaward section of which, the Royalty Fishery, is also a sea-trout water of great productivity. Sea-trout are not pursued as a speciality above the Royalty, but the fish spawn between Christchurch and Ringwood, and some filter through to higher reaches.

The title 'Royalty Fishery' was conferred by royal grant in the reign of Queen Mary and renewed by Elizabeth I in the sixteenth century. The fishery is now owned by Bournemouth & West Hampshire Water, which acquired it in 1929.

The Royalty lies within the Avon Valley Site of Special Scientific Interest and comprises over 1 mile of double-bank water noted for salmon, barbel, pike, chub and bream, many of specimen size. Outstanding in this remarkable company is the sea-trout.

I met Alan Godfrey, Head Bailiff of the Royalty Fishery in the fishery office which overlooks the Royalty water. He first started to fish with his father at the age of seven, and has fished the Hampshire Avon for 29 years. Initially, he began with coarse fish and then added sea-trout and salmon. He has worked at the Royalty for 18 years and is now Head Bailiff with an Assistant Bailiff under him.

He is on duty at all the hours of the day and night. Rods never know when he will appear, and nor do poachers. Illegal netting is the main poaching problem, and he controls it from a boat with the help of his assistant and the Harbour Moorings Bailiff. Their method is to drag a soft metal claw, like an anchor, behind the boat down through Steep Banks, below Bridge Pool, to Mudeford Run, collecting any nets on the way!

Alan's is a busy life, involving advising, regulating, issuing fishing tickets, cutting weed and many other duties. I am indebted to him for showing me the fishery whilst I recorded his gems of angling wisdom.

Look over the road bridge in Christchurch by the King's Arms, the Abbey and the Roman ruins any day between 16 June and 31 October, with the Garden Pool above, and below you, you will see a moored punt of good size and modern construction bearing the name 'Royalty Fishery'. That punt is in the Bridge Pool.

Now glance to the left, at stonework on the bank, from which a pipe emerges a few yards downstream from the bridge. From that pipe to a large willow tree about 200 yd downstream is the outstanding tidal sea-trout pool of central southern England. This pool yields the major share of the Royalty's sea-trout catch, which totals about 2,000 or 3,000 fish per season, the majority of which are returned.

The punt may be occupied by three people, but only two rods are allowed. Rods may start to fish the pool by fly at 6.00 am from the bank, paying due regard to their back cast, which will extend over a public footpath which runs alongside the pool. At 7.00 am rods may go out in the boat to fish through the day with small gilt and marsh worms on trotting tackle (marsh worms inhabit marshland over which fresh water floods at high tide).

The trotting rod should be long, with a gentle action. Alan uses an 11ft 6 in Fred J. Taylor trotting rod by Hardy. The reel is a centre-pin filled with 4-lb nylon. His floats are a speciality, made from riverside reed cut to lengths of 6 or 7 in, with red or yellow painted tops and submerged sections coloured green. Below the float are a few lead-free split shot to sink the worms close to the river bed. Alan ties his hook straight to the reel line, as he considers that a trace of lesser strength, with added knots, adds to the risk of losing fish. Some anglers go down to 3 or even 2 lb, but sea-trout over the expected size will smash such threads to bits.

In the evening, until 11.00 pm when fishing must stop, anglers usually revert to the fly. Fly lines are usually fast-sinking to carry the fly down to the fish in the fast current. If the tide is slack a floating line can be used with good results on warm humid nights. Popular fly patterns include Black & Silver, Alexandra, Dunkeld and Stoat's Tail in tandems of about No 8 hook size or 1-in tubes. Very few anglers use luminous strip or Beta lights on their flies. Leaders are often of 8-lb point strength. Spinning is not allowed.

Being tidal, the ebbs and flows govern the best periods in which to fish. As in Southampton Water there are four tides every 24 hours instead of the two found in other areas. There are about three and a half hours of suitable water on each tide: two hours on the ebb, then one and a half or two hours as the tide back-fills. Fishing is not productive when the water is slack at low tide, but becomes fruitful as fresh sea-liced fish come into the pool as the tide rises. Catches can reach an outstanding total of 80 or 100 sea-trout in 24 hours, but all fish of less than 14 in from the tip of the nose to the fork of the tail must be returned to the water.

A few heavy fish of 7–10 lb enter the river in June; after that numbers increase but weights reduce. In August and September it is not unusual for 40 or 50 fish to be taken each day. The Avon is a late-running river, and sea-trout fishing continues until the end of October, although it ceases with the arrival of the first frosts.

Alan's own heaviest sea-trout weighed 11 lb 8 oz. It was taken from the Bridge Pool on a No 8

Black & Silver tandem on 8-lb nylon in coloured water in August. His rod was a 9-ft Hardy Farnborough No 1 throwing a line of high density. Starting the battle in the boat he had to land and run down the bank after the fish. All his dressed line and most of the backing disappeared in the direction of France, but the fish suddenly came to a stop. On reaching his prize he found that it had fouled the line around a rock and was lying belly up, waiting to be netted.

If you want to fish the Bridge Pool, you should write to the Fishery Manager in February. If you are lucky, you may be allocated a single day – that is, one day in the whole season because the fishing is in great demand. There are no season rods on the Bridge Pool.

The river divides upstream of the Bridge Pool, which is formed by the major western flow. To the east, along the same road, is Waterloo Bridge Pool which is fished from a boat, also by trotting and fly. When I looked over the bridge, I saw fat chub upstream, and below, portmanteaux mullet of 5 or 6 lb.

In October large sea-trout enter this pool. About six years ago an angler caught two sea-trout weighing 13 and 17½ lb, believed to have been enticed by a worm. The numbers of fish taken from this pool are much smaller than from the Bridge Pool but they are of substantial weight.

Since 1996, sea-trout fishing by fly has been offered at night on the main Royalty river on two beats, with two rods on each, between 21 June and 31 October, from half an hour after sunset to 6.00 am.

Crossing the footbridge below Alan's office we turned upstream and there, on a shallow, were many sea-trout basking in the sun. At Knapp Mill, famed for the Parlour salmon pool, there is a narrow sea-trout pass on the left bank, allowing passage to the river above the mill. This pass leads to two pipes which are open to view and both of which, on my visit, held numerous first-return schoolies. The sea-trout passage is in addition to

The Parlour. The salmon pass is on the left beneath Knapp Mill; the sea-trout pass is the small slot in the wall on the right of the photograph at water level

the salmon pass alongside the right bank and leading under the mill.

Both Knapp Mill and the Weir are equipped with salmon passes and counters; the electronic equipment not only records numbers of salmon and sea-trout moving upstream, but takes a photograph of each. The pictures are automatically extruded from the machine and, on my visit, showed that eight fish had passed the Weir counter in the last two days of August 1996. In the same period, which coincided with a spring tide, 31 salmon, grilse and sea-trout passed through the Knapp Mill counter on one night, and 16 on the next.

Below the Weir is Edward's, a small pool, but one of the most prolific salmon pools on the river. I remember my father-in-law taking a 14-lb salmon there in the 1970s. The fly pattern was probably a Thunder & Lightning, his favourite. At that time, being in his 70s, he was somewhat less athletic than me and not inclined to chase

hooked fish. One day, when he was fishing from the left bank, he hooked a double-figure fish in the Parlour. This salmon, as he put it, 'took-off for the sea'. Taking the fly rod from him (for even when fishing the worm he used a 12 ft 6 in Sharpe's), I chased it downstream, crossed the river and landed it from the far bank.

The Tamar and the Lyd, Devon/Cornwall Border

The Tamar rises near the northern Devon/Cornwall border approximately 6 miles above Tamar Lake, the reservoir through which it flows; the east bank of the lake is in Devon, the west in Cornwall. It then continues to form the county boundary whilst flowing south past Launceston. In the region of that town it is joined by the River Lyd, and the Carey, Thrushel, Wolf and Ottery streams. The River Inny joins forces with the Tamar below Launceston. The river then continues southwards to a joint estuary with the River Tavy in Plymouth Sound.

Tamar water is more opaque than that of its tributary the Lyd, which rises on Dartmoor north of Tavistock and to the east of Lydford. After heavy rain the Tamar, which runs through agricultural land, becomes coloured and unfishable, sometimes for three days or more; the Lyd, by contrast, clears rapidly as a spate runs off.

Otters are common on the Lyd and are sometimes seen hunting by day as well as at dusk and at night. They cause little disturbance if they pass through a pool. If they stop to fish for bullheads, loach or grayling at night one has little chance at scared fish.

The birdlife is superb: kingfishers, dippers, wagtails fluttering after waterborne flies as they hatch, and buzzards mewing overhead, are all common. Sometimes there is the excitement of a peregrine taking a pigeon, and sparrowhawks are not rare. There are many badgers in the valley and they may be seen as one drives home after a night on the river – they seem unconcerned by the headlights of a car.

Higher up the valley, where I lived for 15 years in an isolated farmhouse, are roe and red deer, the latter with superb heads owing to the rich feeding on the vegetation of this loveliest of valleys.

Both rivers provide good harvests of salmon and sea-trout. Sea-trout on their second, third

The Hampshire Avon is also a noted coarse fishery. Here, a rod is playing a 10½-lb barbel in the Parlour. The sea-trout pass is just visible on the left

The fish counter at the Weir on the Royalty. Fish are counted and photographed as they pass upstream – see strip of prints being ejected on the right of the machine.

and subsequent spawning runs enter the river and are caught from early June onwards, with school peal, the first-time spawners, arriving in July, usually after the first full moon of that month and the consequent high spring tide.

Salmon reach the middle Tamar and the lower end of the Lyd in May. Surprisingly, in the most recent two seasons, two sea-winter salmon of 9–13 lb have arrived in good numbers some miles up the river earlier than usual in May and June.

For sea-trout the best months are July and August; the greatest number of salmon are caught in September and the first two weeks of October. The open seasons are 1 March–14 October for salmon and 3 March–30 September for sea-trout.

Sea-trout start spawning in the heads of the streams at the end of October; salmon spawn between mid-November and mid-December. After two or three years their smolts go down to the estuary between March and May – early if there are spates, and not until late April and May if there is a prolonged dry spell.

The tidal area below Gunnislake is 18 miles downstream of the Lyd, yet sea-liced peal can be caught at the Arundel Arms water on that river within 48 hours of the fish leaving the tide, particularly schoolies. On my visit on 11 July 1996, the hotel waters that season had yielded about two dozen salmon, of which three-quarters were sea-liced. Without doubt, spring tides bring in fresh peal at the time of a full moon, and these yielding good catches on the Arundel water one week later as the moon wanes and dark nights arrive. These silvery fish darken in colour after a few weeks and become much more difficult to catch than when fresh run. Fly-fishing is the only method permitted on the Arundel water on the Lyd unless there is a huge spate and the river is too coloured to fish the fly. Spinning is then allowed, but only until the river clears.

Roy Buckingham started to fish the Tamar in 1957. He has keepered and fished at the Arundel since 1969, and many guests have benefitted from his guidance. We met at Jock Scott Pool on the River Lyd, where all the pools of the hotel stretch are named after salmon flies. The water was at the low level suitable for night sea-trout fishing on the day of my visit, and would need to rise by 1 ft to become fishable for salmon. When I examined the pool in mid-afternoon I could see a shoal of peal in the middle, where the water is about 4 or

5 ft deep. At dusk some of these fish move to shallower areas in the tail of the pool, to be joined by others skittering up the river through the rocky shallows which divide deeper areas.

Roy's rod is a 9-ft or 9 ft 6 in carbon fibre by Orvis, rated AFTM No 6, with a Hardy Sunbeam 3½-in reel which is set at a light drag, braking being provided by Roy's finger on the fly line. Both rods have an easy action to absorb the shock of a smash take. He uses a white floating fly line. A sinking or sink-tip line would catch the fly on the bedrock of the river, which is not deep. A sinking fly line in the second half of the night, as has been advocated elsewhere, is not an option on the Lyd.

The fly line may be weight-forward or double-tapered; either is suitable because casting is over such short distances in the narrow Lyd that neither is superior to the other. Roy's 9-ft leader is of Maxima Chameleon, half of the length being 25-lb breaking strain, then tapering down steeply to an 8-lb point through several reducing sections joined by blood knots. Sometimes he uses a knotless tapered 10-lb salmon leader, adding an 8-lb point.

He fishes three flies at night: on the point a large fly on a Partridge long-shank lure hook, size 4 or 6; on the middle dropper a size 8; and a size 10 or 12 on the top dropper. If he wants to fish a little more deeply, an aluminium tube of 1 or 1¼ in, or at most 1½ in, with a Partridge No 10 outpoint treble or a Waddington, is used at the point. The hook of the tube is kept in line with a rubber sleeve, the Waddington treble by 25-lb nylon whipped to the treble shank and the wire of the Waddington body. He does not use a Beta light on his flies, but sometimes ties in two pieces of luminous strip, cut in the shape of jungle cock eyes, one on each side. These strips are activated by shining a torch on them just before use, and seem to be at their most effective as the glow starts to fade.

By using three flies, Roy caters both for nights when peal will only take large flies and those when they prefer small ones. By fishing a selection of sizes, he avoids having to change them. The point fly is usually a hairy black Bumble devised by his colleague David Pilkington. The hook is a long-shank streamer single, size 4 or size 6, and the dressing is a slim body of black floss ribbed oval silver tinsel, black palmered hackle, and a teal flank feather wound on as a hackle at the throat, the silk being black Naples. His favourite team of flies is: point, the Bumble on a size 4 hook; first dropper, a Silver Invicta; top dropper, a Jungle Alexandra.

With two droppers there is a risk that a trailing fly may catch in a snag whilst a fish is being played. This may be overcome if a fish takes the top dropper by using a knotless tapered leader and tying the dropper extensions tightly against the leader with a tucked half blood knot. If the top dropper is taken it will slide down to the tail fly, pushing the middle fly down at the same time. If the middle dropper is taken it will slide down to the point, just leaving the top fly which is, to a limited extent, out of the way.

A net should be carried when fishing this stretch, particularly for large peal, since there are few beaches on which to strand them. Torches must be used with care, and the reflector covered with red cellophane. Roy advises beginners to be stealthy and regain their hunting instincts. He suggests that they imagine they are the fish, quietly moving in mid-river, sipping down a fly. Suddenly, there is a great splash as a fly line crashes down on the water surface, or a heavy boot kicks over a stone. Panic ensues and the word is passed in the shoal that anglers have arrived. Watch the stealthy foot movements of a heron, which has neither flashing eyes nor boots on its feet.

There are three places in Jock Scott Pool from which to cast at night: high on the bank at the top of the pool, but only when it is pitch dark, as one is outlined against the sky; off rocks halfway down the pool; and off a shingle bank just above the tail. Never start to fish until the leaves cannot be seen on the trees on the far bank.

The pool is almost 20 yd long, but only 12–15 yd wide. In consequence, only short casts are possible. Roy advises anglers to make their first cast with one rod's length of line outside the top ring, casting this up, up and across, across, and then down and across the river. Then they should pull off another yard of line from the reel and repeat that casting arc. In due course the width of the river will be covered. In the first two sequences there is no need to retrieve line; raising the rod tip is sufficient recovery and movement of the fly. On the third pull from the reel, start recovering by hand with the rod tip close to the water and at an angle to the line on the surface. This angle allows the rod to bend on a hard take by a strong peal, acting as a shock absorber to prevent the leader snapping.

Because the river is heavily bushed in some places, a roll cast may be necessary. Some anglers who are used to lake and reservoir fishing cast too far when starting to cover a pool, thus frightening the peel by letting the line cross their vision window before they have a chance to see and take the fly.

Sometimes large brown trout are taken at night when they come to the shallows to feed on minnows and trout and salmon fry. The largest, of 3 lb 1 oz, was taken on the Thrushel. A scale reading showed that it was 18 years of age. The Arundel has no rule that school peal must be returned; the size limit is 7 in, the same as for brown trout. The decision is left to individual anglers, but Roy considers it a shame to kill the smallest fish, which may be no more than ½ lb.

His largest sea-trout, of nearly 6 lb, was taken in late June about 500 yd below Hartley Weir on the Lyd. The fly was a 1-in plastic tube with a gold-ribbed black body and a wing of squirrel tail dyed black.

Fishing a surface lure at night is a favourite method. There is no better lure than a greased Muddler minnow skated fast across the river to create a wake. The leader is degreased and the droppers remain in position. Those droppers give one an extra chance; they are often taken after the Muddler has attracted a fish by the disturbance it creates on the water surface. Sometimes the Muddler will hook all the fish which chase it. On other nights there are just pulls and no fish. These false takes may happen time after time, and there seems no solution. Even adding a flying treble hook does not help.

Whilst I was watching the shoal in Jock Scott Pool a peal made a movement which often reveals the presence of previously unseen fish – there was a silver flash as it turned on its side. I asked Roy if sea-trout could be caught by day on the fly in low water. He said that silver-flanked peal are usually fresh run and may take a fly, but they are so wary that great care must be taken both in one's approach and in one's use of fine tackle. It is necessary to use a floating fly line coupled to a 15-ft leader tapered from 25 lb at the butt to 3 lb at the point, and degreased along the entire length. This leader can be made of several sections of reducing strength nylon, each section being about 4 lb less than the one before. Thus, six or seven sections are required. Another method of constructing a suitable leader is to take a 9-ft Platil knotless tapered leader for salmon with a 10-lb point and add two 1-yd sections of 6-lb and 3-lb breaking strain.

The fly should have some weight. His preference is for a No 14 Esmond Drury treble hook with a fine copper wire body. To this he adds wisps of squirrel tail dyed black on each side. A modern invention is also effective: a No 10, No 12 or No 14 Gold Head nymph.

The approach is from downstream, like nymph fishing for chalk-stream trout. The fly is cast up and pitched about 1 yd above the shoal, allowed to sink, then raised in front of it by lifting the top of the rod. Two or three fish usually follow and may, take. The process is fascinating, a Hiawatha stalk and Oliver-Kite-induced take rolled into one.

When the water is clearing as a spate goes down, but there is still a stain in the river, sea-trout may be caught in daylight in the tails of pools by using a standard reservoir lure cast downstream. Attractors such as Sweeney Todd and Viva are suitable.

The Border Esk, English/Scottish Border

The Esk is formed from the Black and White Esk rivers. The Black Esk flows south from Black Esk Reservoir which is fed by five streams in Eskdalemuir Forest. The White Esk catchment comprises many rivulets which rise in the Ettrick Hills. It flows south, whilst the river Ettrick flows north-east out of the hills and ultimately joins the river Tweed to flow into the North Sea. The Esk enters the Solway Firth on the west coast.

At the confluence of the Black and White Esks, 13 miles north-west of Langholm as the crow flies, is the King Pool in a gorge. Above this pool the White Esk is controlled by the Forestry Commission, with fishing tickets available from the Hart Manor Hotel in Eskdalemuir.

Below the confluence, down to Enzieholm Bridge, the river is under the control of Tanlawhill Estates (see 'Finding Sea-trout Fishing' at the end of the book.). Below Enzieholm Bridge are private fisheries, but at Bentpath Tony King arranges fishing down to Burnfoot from Westerhall Estates (see 'Finding Sea-trout Fishing'). From Burnfoot Bridge down past Craig to Craig Hill, fishing is available from Craig Farm on the right bank.

The river now enters the Esk and Liddle Fisheries which are owned by the Buccleuch Estates. This ownership continues to the English border, with the exception of a left-bank section south of Langholm which belongs to Broomholm Estates. Broomholm water runs from Skipper's Bridge down to the confluence with the Tarras Water which enters the Esk from the north-east. Also below Skipper's Bridge is water fished by the Langholm Association. Details of the Esk and Liddle Fisheries are contained in the section 'Finding Sea-trout Fishing'. They consist of the Langholm and Canonbie beats on the Esk, and the Newcastleton and Lower Liddle fisheries on the Liddle Water, the main tributary of the Esk. Buccleuch Estates also let six private beats on a weekly basis, allowing three rods on each beat.

The sea-trout season is from 1 May to 30 September, and the salmon season from 1 February to 31 October. If there is a good flow, there are likely to be sea-trout in the 4–6-lb bracket at the start of the season. The run increases until August, whilst the average weight reduces to the region of 2 lb. First-return fish, called finnock in the Highlands and herling on the Esk, appear in July and August.

Anthony King of the Esk and Borders Guiding Service is a fly-fishing instructor and angling guide registered by the Register of Experienced Fly-Fishing Instructors and Schools (REFFIS). He also holds the Instructor qualifications of the Salmon and Trout Association (STANIC) and the Scottish Anglers' National Association (SANA). He lives immediately above the Esk at Bentpath, 16 miles upstream of the sea, and has fished the river for 19 seasons.

He usually fishes for sea-trout with an 11-ft single-handed rod. The reel is a 3½-in James Young multiplier on which he uses a green Wetcel Intermediate sinking line for most water conditions. His leaders are Hardy's Copolymer knotless tapered to 12 lb, to the end of which he attaches 4 ft of 8-lb monofilament. The tapered leader and tippet are joined by a four-turn water knot, the downward-pointing end being used to form a dropper. The whole leader is therefore 13 ft in length. His net is a Pelican 24-in metal bowframe, designed for grilse and salmon.

Tony showed me a photograph of a sea-trout of over 5 lb which he had caught early in 1996 on the outfit described above. On that night the point fly, which it took, was a Butcher, and the dropper was a Dark Mackerel with red Lurex body, claret hackle and mallard wing. He likes a substantial dropper which will make some disturbance on the water surface. The fish came from the Skelly Hole on the Canonbie Beat, so called because it used to hold a shoal of chub, called skelly in Scotland.

He ties his flies on with a two-turn Turle knot to keep them in line with the leader, then goes to the throat of the pool he is fishing. Standing in the stickle, well above the throat, he casts straight down into the throat, then moves the rod to his left and his right to cover the whole entrance. The next move is to the neck where he again makes downstream casts. As the flow slows in the centre and tail of the pool he tweaks the line to give it extra movement. He experiments with flies, dressing his own in a wonderfully muddled wood-lined room which gave me the impression of a happy angler. The river runs below his old stone house, so close that he only has to walk a few yards to see his water-level marker stone in the river (see photograph).

Tony is dedicated to the fly. Worming and spinning are in any case only allowed on the Esk in certain places and at high-water levels. I decided to concentrate on fly in this Esk account.

The following are some of the creations in which he has put his trust.

The Snake
This fly is 3 in in overall length. A No 12 round-eye outpoint treble hook is at the tail, held in line

REFFIS instructor Tony King's water-level gauge. The white lines are at 6-in intervals. LS stands for 'low summer'. Tony comments: 'If the water is at the bottom I will be gardening; if on the top, fishing'.

Contrast a winter flood with low summer. Tony is standing in a depression above the river bank in which he has twice found stranded salmon.

with the single hook at the head by three 2-in strands of 15-lb Maxima nylon. Over the three-strand body a plastic tube, the covering of an electric wire, is slid on and heated with a hair dryer. The heat shrinks the plastic tightly onto the monofilament strands. The tube is then covered with silver Mylar tubing. The wing, which extends beyond the treble hook, is of any hair or feather, to which is mixed some Flashabou. The whole resembles a small fish or elver and is fished off a slow-sinking or sink-tip line.

The Steve Parton hooked fly

This is dressed on a No 6 nickel silver Steve Parton single-lure hook, although the word 'dressed' is an exaggeration. A bunch of black or black and white Marabou is tied in with black silk at the head, the shank of the silver hook being left undressed. When the Marabou is chewed off by the sea-trout, a replacement tuft is tied on.

Tail Nippers' fly

This is dressed on a long-shanked No 6 or No 8 single Low Water salmon fly hook. It is used when there are many stale fish in the river which Tony calls 'tail nippers'. These he wishes to return to the water, and they are more easily released from a single hook than a treble. The rear half of the shank above the bend is left bare, while the front half is covered by flat silver tinsel. The wing is

Standing above the throat of a pool at night, the rod is swung from the right to . . .

. . . the left.

teal flank feather, and the throat hackle red or magenta hen.

His favourite dropper is a small bushy creation on a No 12 hook, which resembles a shrimp. The fly has a red tinsel body ribbed over with fine copper wire. The hackle is claret, and the wing is brown hair or mallard flank feather. Being bushy, the fly skates on the water surface.

Of the classic patterns the Medicine style is a reliable confidence booster. The Butcher has a touch of red which does well in coloured water. A No 12 Teal & Silver Blue takes fish in low water when knotted to thin Orvis Super Strong tippet nylon. Tony uses a tiny Muddler-style fly, resembling a Black Muddler, with clipped deer hair head, when there is little water in the river and a lot of algae on the rocks. The head makes the fly

slightly buoyant in the booby manner, lifting it over the boulders.

The Spey, Scotland

The Spey rises 1,500 ft above sea level, close to the miniature Loch Spey near Melgarve in the Corrieyairack Forest. This is on the south side of the Monadhliath Mountains, 14 miles west of Dalwhinnie. It then runs east, close to the track of General Wade's road to Laggan Bridge. There, it turns north-east to pass Newtonmore, Kingussie, Kincraig, Aviemore, Boat of Garten and Grantown-on-Spey. It then continues north-east to Aberlour where it turns north by Rothes and Fochabers to Spey Bay in the Moray Firth. It has the second largest catchment in Scotland with a number of tributaries: the

Kurt Conroy Spey casting under Old Spey Bridge.

Trium, the Calder, the Alt Mor, the Tromie, the Feshie, the Druie, the Nethy, the Dulnain, the Avon (which is pronounced 'A' an'), and the Fiddich.

Like the skiers at Aviemore, anglers hope for a plentiful fall of snow in winter. This accumulates in the Monadhliath, Grampian, Badenoch and Cairngorm mountain corries. Snow melt then feeds the Spey through spring and early summer, ensuring a good flow down the main river, which is not obstructed by natural or man-made barriers. Salmon, grilse and sea-trout thus spread readily though the river.

At the end of the 1993 season the net and coble fisheries ceased operations. This did not lead at once to the expected increase in rod catches of salmon and sea-trout. The Spey District Fishery Board statistics show the 1994 catch as a percentage of the long-term mean as follows:

Spring salmon	Summer salmon	Grilse	Salmon & grilse	Sea-trout
30%	116%	256%	130%	149%

However, it is pleasing to be able to report that statistics made available to me by the Strathspey Angling Improvement Association (SAIA) at Grantown show that 1996 yielded the highest sea-trout catch to rods on the Association waters since the nets came off, a total of about 1,300 fish. This compares with 388 in 1995 and 657 in 1994.

The river is usually split into upper, middle and lower waters: the upper from the source to Boat of Garten, the middle roughly from Grantown to Aberlour, and the lower from Craigellachie Hotel water to Fochabers and the sea.

The open season for both salmon and sea-trout is from 11 February to 30 September. Long sections of the river are fished by members and visitor ticket holders of different angling associations. There are about 13 of these, of which SAIA is the largest. It is usually a condition that visitors wishing to fish an association water stay at guest-houses or hotels within that region.

SAIA has 4 miles of the Spey River from Broomhill Bridge down to Grantown road bridge. Members and holders of seven-day visitors tickets also fish 1¼ miles of Upper Castle Grant water on Thursdays, Fridays and Saturdays. In addition, SAIA holds 12 miles of the River Dulnain from Inverlaidnan Bridge to its junction with the Spey downstream of Dulnain Bridge. Tickets for the Strathspey are available only from Mortimer's shop in Grantown High Street; Grant Mortimer is the Secretary and Treasurer of the Association. Tickets for visitors, who are warmly welcomed to the district, are issued in the following categories: season, seven days (excluding Sundays), seven days junior, three days and one day. A seven-day ticket starting on a Monday allows the holder to fish the following Monday as well, likewise Tuesday to Tuesday, and so on. Holders of three-day and one-day tickets, which are available for use on Thursday, Friday and Saturday only, are not allowed to fish on Upper Castle Grant; holders of seven-day and season tickets can fish that water on those days.

Tickets for other associations are usually available in local towns in the Spey valley. A useful fishing publication is issued free of charge by the Grantown Tourist Office in the High Street. There are also many private beats, and the means of access to some of these is given in the section 'Finding Sea-trout Fishing' at the end of the book.

The Spey is a wide, strong river. It must be fished with due regard to the safety of yourself and others. The Spey Fishing Trust Ltd and Spey District Fishery Board have made recommendations, of which the following is a selection:

1.   Take care to keep rods and lines away from overhead power lines.
2.   Wear a hat and glasses when casting in a strong wind, and do not cast over the upstream shoulder in a strong downstream wind.

3. Be aware of any obstructions, and people behind, when casting.

4. Stop fishing and move well away from the rod in an electric storm.

5. When wading:

    a) Wear an approved buoyancy aid (see photograph).

    b) Do not tie chest waders at the waist.

    c) Use a wading staff (see photograph).

    d) Do not move one foot until the other is firmly settled.

    e) Try not to wade against the current.

On parts of the river a lifejacket or buoyancy aid is obligatory. Lara Bingham points with her left hand to the red toggle which perforates a gas cylinder to inflate the jacket. The strap on her right forefinger should be attached to a belt.

    f) If you fall in, turn on your back with head upstream and gradually paddle in towards the bank and shallow water. Crawl onto the bank and empty your waders by lying on your back with your feet in the air.

    g) Be ready to help anyone who is in difficulties.

I met Colonel (retd) Tom D. Hawkins MBE, President of SAIA, in his office behind Mortimer's fishing tackle shop. He caught his first sea-trout in the river Nith in Dumfriesshire at the age of 12, and has always taken every opportunity to have a fly rod in his hand. These chances have been limited by 40 years in the army, but he usually managed an annual visit to the Spey.

His best sea-trout came in March when spinning for salmon on a private beat on Castle Grant, and weighed 7 lb 2 oz. It was unusually early in the season.

A few sea-trout enter the river the April, but the first realistic runs are in May. These increase in June, and coincide in July with the arrival of grilse. Sea-trout continue to enter in August, but the run tails off rapidly in September when the main entry of finnock takes place. These first-return little sea-trout are put back into the river by adults, but junior anglers of 15 years and under may retain one or two. By the time finnock have arrived at Grantown, most of the large sea-trout have departed upstream. The average weight throughout the season (excluding finnock) is almost exactly 2½ lb. Many are sea-liced, as are salmon. Tom considers that sea-lice may stay on fish for up to a week, as they take several days to reach the SAIA waters in a cold spring.

As I have said snow melt has a profound effect on the river Spey. It may continue into June, keeping water temperatures in the 40–50°F bracket. This leads anglers to use sinking fly lines as well as floaters in their sea-trout fishing.

The association allows all methods other than prawn, shrimp and maggot. Maggots are thus not allowed on a fly hook. Float fishing is banned, as is the use of lead-cored fly lines. Worm fishing is only permitted when the river is 6 in or more above summer level (see photograph of water marker). On Upper Castle Grant 'fly only' is the rule.

There is a noticeable movement towards fish conservation on the river. This leads to increased use of the fly, and the return of fish towards the end of the season. Ten years ago it was common to see anglers with spinning rods and tins of worms. This is now a rare sight. The gaff, although it is legal from May to the end of the season, is now also seldom seen. It is a rule of SAIA that fish may not be sold. Care of the river and the fish leads to care in personal attitude: stealth, a quiet approach, felt-soled waders and the wearing of unobtrusive clothing.

The Spey is a big river, holding a fair number of large sea-trout. It was thus not surprising to learn that Tom fishes at night with a 12-ft double-handed fly rod to give more control of casting and the fish. As to reels, he is spoilt by the proximity of Mortimer's shop, and uses Hardy Sovereigns, Ultralite and Marquis disc.

His fly line in summer is a floater, used with braided leaders of varying densities, all greater than water to prevent the fly skating and vary the depth at which it is worked. The tippet is of Maxima Chameleon at a breaking strain of 10 or 12 lb. His favourite fly is a Jay & Silver on a No 6 Low Water single salmon hook. This fly has a blae wing from the primaries of a jay, and a silver body.

Successful patterns on the river, as on other waters, have silver bodies and black wings. Tom finds that a large single hook takes a firm hold in the jaw of the fish, whilst small hooks often pull out of the soft mouths of sea-trout. An innovation is the addition of an Aerolight in a tiny ⅛-in plastic tube which he shrinks onto the hook shank. The light is supposed to last for ten years, and its glow is a help in locating the fish when the time comes to net it on the water surface, and in locating others which have been placed upon the bank.

The river has many boulders, which make wading hazardous at night. Tom usually nets his

The water gauge above Spey Bridge. River Watcher Alistair Grant is pointing at the level above which rods may fish with a worm.

fish whilst wading, and then goes cautiously to the bank. At one time he strung them on a cord, pushing a wooden toggle through the gills, but was discouraged when an otter seized the lot. He has a golden rule with his car keys: they go in a pocket *inside* his waders.

One night when fishing on the river Nith he did very well when a full moon kept shining through scudding clouds. On the Spey he likes it to be pitch black. So dark was it one night that he became disorientated whilst circumnavigating several boulders, and ended up casting to his own bank. At night it is wise to wear a buoyancy aid or life jacket. This is a requirement when fishing Upper Castle Grant, and many anglers take this precaution elsewhere on SAIA waters.

Alistair Grant or Ally, as he is known to all, is the SAIA River Watcher, and was born in Grantown. He took this position nine years ago, following in the footsteps of his father. As a watcher he does not have the power of arrest conferred on a water bailiff, although his duties are very similar. He is well placed to keep an eye on things, living within 100 yd of the river. Visitors would be well advised to seek his advice, for he knows the waters like the back of his hand.

He caught his first sea-trout at the age of nine. His best was 7½ lb taken on the Long Pool on the SAIA beats on the River Dalnain 25 years ago. This fell to a Toby when he was spinning for salmon in August.

Ally accompanied Tom and me on a tour of SAIA waters, pointing out hot spots for salmon and sea-trout. He showed me the water-level marker board above Spey Bridge where summer level is marked. He makes the level known to rods, ensuring that fly only is fished in certain areas in low water, and in full river conditions advising when one may fish a worm.

Just below Old Spey Bridge I had a long conversation with Willy Stirrat, who has fished the SAIA waters for 20 years. His first visit was on an Easter weekend, when he caught finnock. I was surprised that they were there at that time, but Willy is adamant that finnock used to run in late at the end of the season and overwinter in the river; although he doubted that they spawned. In the last decade he has come back mainly for the sea-trout, starting his fly season during the first week in June. In May the water is higher, sea-

trout are running through in batches and the worm is a good bait in a full river. In early June he hopes the water temperature will be 12°C. (52°F), when the fly comes in to play for sea-trout, and the floating line for salmon.

His night fly line is a floater with a slow-sinking braided leader and an 8-ft, 8-lb monofilament tippet. In the first two weeks of June his favourite fly for both salmon and sea-trout is a No 10 Logie, on either a double or a treble hook. He does not care for droppers because of the risk of snagging.

Willy's favourite pool is Lurg, in the tail, off the green bank. But if the water level is 6 in above summer level he does not brother to fish at night, as the river is too high.

He chooses a 15-ft double-handed fly rod of easy action for the night. This enables him to fish small flies 25 yd out in the middle of the river, covering water other rods are unable to reach. Spey casting is necessary in many parts of the river, even at night. Sometimes, in low-water conditions, he may reduce to a 12-ft single-handed rod. In slow-running water he sometimes makes the cast slightly upstream, allowing the current to work the fly line round into a belly. This tactic speeds up the fly and is attractive to sea-trout. The surface lure does not account for many fish.

It is profitable to fish right through the night. Sea-trout may 'go down' for short periods, but that is the time to have a cup of tea before starting to fish again until dawn. Then there is always the chance of a salmon if one changes to a 12-lb leader and a slightly larger fly. Willy has taken many salmon in this way, probably unsettled fish which have arrived in the night.

When sea-trout are running he sometimes fishes for them by day if the water is high in summer. 'Down and across' is the method, a good one for both sea-trout and salmon.

The 1996 season was a good one. Willy stopped fishing for sea-trout at the end of August, having taken 100 fish. He then caught one more of 3 lb

The Dulnain at Carrbridge.

when he was after salmon. Being a good specimen he kept it, making 101. In a normal season he anticipates a total of about 50 fish.

His best bag on a single night was nine fish averaging 2½ lb – he did not lose one. In early July, however, many came unstuck after giving a good solid pull at the fly. There seems to be no explanation for this difference.

Willy recounts the following experience:

> I was standing on a platform one night when I saw something coming along the side of it. I shone my light and saw an otter under the water; it looked just like a porpoise. It swam by my feet, hauled out onto the platform and sat down not 3 ft from me. I still had the torch on it whilst it gave itself a good scratch. It then gave a wee look at me and slid back into the river.

I was privileged to be given a sight of Willy's secret weapon, but no photograph was to be taken. It is called the Swallowtail, and is in three parts to a total length of ¾ in, excluding the No 14 treble hook. The head is tied on a small plastic bead, a tuft of black bear hair sticking out on each side (like a Stoat's Tail), mixed with two or three strands of bucktail dyed yellow. The body is ⅛ in of thin aluminium tube, bare, threaded onto the nylon leader, which passes through the bead and then the tube; both sit on the eye of the treble hook.

Bear hair is stiff. It sticks out at 45 degrees on both sides. The fibres of the tails of stoats and squirrels are too soft. It seemed to me that these protruding wings, one on each side, would make a slight disturbance in the current. When the water is low and warm he takes off his braided leader and fishes the Swallowtail off 10 ft of nylon on a floating line.

David Herbert a SAIA rod and angling guide at Grantown is aged 18 years. He is keen and competently operates an angling guide service for trout, sea-trout and salmon from Parkburn Guest House, Grantown. His guide qualification was awarded by the register of Experienced Fly Fishing Instructors and Schools (REFFIS), of which his late father was an Instructor member.

He hooked his first salmon of 5 lb at the age of four on the river Nairn. He immediately handed the rod, which was not of the highest quality, to his father, but it fell apart. The fish was then played and landed off the reel. His second fish, of 12 lb, came from the same river at the age of nine on a spinner. He caught his first sea-trout on the fly on the Grantown water at the age of nine, in the Tarric Mor pool. His fly rod was an AFTM No 6, 9 ft long. The team of three flies had a Silver Stoat on the point with two Hawthorns as droppers, with the intention of taking brown trout.

On 29 August 1996 he had what must be the morning of a lifetime. The fish he extracted from Poll Caich Pool on that morning will be very hard for him to equal, let alone exceed.

With a 9-ft rod, a floating fly line to which he attached a 2-ft cut-down slow-sinking braided leader, he knotted on a nylon leader tapered from 18 lb to a 6-lb point. Two droppers were formed. With this outfit he fished 'down and across' by day for brown trout. A Frenchman was fishing for salmon, in view and above him.

After five casts he caught a brown trout of just over 2 lb. Five minutes later he took a 1½-lb sea-trout. Both these fish took the same dropper. He

REFFIS Guide David Herbert cuts his silhouette against the skyline, an essential precaution when fishing at night.

dressed the fly himself directly onto a No 16 Esmond Drury treble; the body was flat pearl tinsel and the wing was stoat's tail. The point fly was a long-shanked treble of a design shown to him by a fishing guest, Steve Parton: a flat pearl tinsel body, wings of stoat's tail and jungle cock cheeks. David christened the fly the Angry Stoat.

After taking these two fish he moved upstream and fished the pool above for half an hour. Returning to Poll Caich at about 1 pm he hooked a solid object. After a few minutes it moved slightly, leading him to believe he had hooked a piece of wood or a branch. But when it moved at speed, his opinion changed! One hour later he had a stale cock salmon of over 30 lb on the bank, having tailed it by hand. The Frenchman hurried down to weigh it in a sling suspended below some scales. These only went to 30 lb, but he estimated the fish at 35 lb.

David returned the salmon to the water, holding it head to current, and it wandered away. He then returned home and went to bed, utterly exhausted. Meanwhile, the catch was confirmed to the River Watcher, Ally, and in Mortimer's shop by the Frenchman.

Norman Stone, the Ghillie, at Revack Estate, Kincardine has always lived in Scotland, where he started to fish at the age of seven. His first sea-trout came from the Spey when he was aged 11, and weighed 3¼ lb; it fell in July to a Teal & Silver on the Strathspey waters at Grantown. His best fish of 7½ lb also took a fly in 1992.

Norman uses a slow-sinking line and works the fly in a figure-of-eight retrieve; he has most faith in a Silver Stoat with jungle cock eyes, and usually dresses this on a No. 8 hook.

His heaviest bag of several fish one night weighed 32 lb. Normally, his rod is an 11-ft

It takes two and a half hours for a spate to travel 8 miles down the river Dulnain from Carrbridge to opposite Muckrach Lodge Hotel. These photographs show that the river rose by about 9 in in 50 minutes. A spate heralds the start of worming and a temporary halt to night sea-trout fly-fishing.

single-handed Bruce & Walker Century. He uses 6-lb nylon, straight off the spool, about 6 or 7 ft in length, and is fished off a slow-sinking fly line. The leader is attached by a short piece of 20-lb nylon needle-knotted into the end of the fly line. The 20-lb nylon and the leader are then joined loop to loop.

He rarely fishes a dry fly by day for sea-trout. He has tried dapping without success, and the surface lure at night has not proved irresistible. There is no doubt Norman relies on fishing the method which produces substantial results – the sub-surface lure.

In June and July sea-trout fishing on the Kincardine water starts at about 11.30 pm. The pools are left untouched by day, and rods meet in the fishing hut for a cup of coffee at 10.30 pm. They understand this arrangement, which is aimed solely at sea-trout if the water is low.

Clearly, if the river rises, the system is rapidly changed, and attention switches to salmon by day.

The estate water is 1.8 miles of right bank with 14 named pools. This length is divided into two sections: Beat A at the top, and Beat B at the lower end, starting at the fishing hut. The estate owns the right bank, while the left is held by Strathspey Estates. Both estates fish both sides, crossing by boat. Thus one fishes Beat A from either bank whilst the other fishes Beat B from either side, the beats being changed over daily at 1 pm.

Sea-trout arrive at this beat above Grantown in the second half of May; June and July are prime months. The average weight is just short of 3 lb. The water has yielded up to 787 off both banks in a season, but 1996 was an average year at a little over 400 fish. In 1995 they took a fish of 10¾ lb, and a lady took four sea-trout one June night of 4¼, 6¼, 6¾ and 10¾ lb. In July the size reduces.

The river at Kincardine. Sea-trout rest under the trees.

Half a dozen fish taken then might weigh 13 or 14 lb. Norman recalled, 'I had one man this year who took eight sea-trout weighing 16 lb. Exactly 2 lb each. It was as though they had come out of a factory.'

He hates the moon and does not like fishing in a mist which in Scotland is called a haar. Low water is needed for the best results. Snow melt keeps the temperature down, but on 20 May 1992 the temperature of the water was 57°F, on 21 May it was down to 54°F, but by 2 June it had risen to 62°F. That was a time of fantastic catches, but even at those temperatures rods used slow-sinking fly lines. Very few finnock reach Norman's water during the season, and if any are caught they are returned.

Bookings to fish on this water should be made through the Revack Estate Office. They are usually for one week, but shorter periods are sometimes available at short notice.

Loch Hope, Sutherland

The way north to Loch Hope is via Lairg and Altnaharra, where there is a hotel of the same name. This outpost of civilization, and sea-trout-anglers' Mecca, is the last place with petrol pumps and roads where two cars can pass each other other than at special passing places. The A836 beyond to Tongue is thus suitable for only one car at a time. The surfaced track north-west, which branches off ½ mile north of the hotel and leads to Loch Hope, was clearly designed by Celts bent upon surprising and attacking their neighbours. The Ordnance Survey describes the 25 miles of that road – it has no name or number –

as being 'generally more than 4 m wide'. This is true, but only just. The cartographer does not mention the surprised wildlife – red deer and grouse – which delighted me as I swooped from summit to summit, bumped around corners, crossed burns and trundled by red-berried rowan trees. A small covey of four grouse, picking up grit from the edge of the road, were not inclined to allow me passage. I took a photograph through the windscreen before they moved off and were hidden by the heather on the verge.

Another half-dozen miles and there rose Dun Dornaigil Broch beside the Strathmore River which, together with its tributaries, feeds Loch Hope. A broch is described in the Concise Oxford Dictionary as 'a prehistoric stone tower in North Scotland and adjacent islands'. Enemies of the inhabiting family had to enter on their knees through a single hole in the thick circular wall. They were thus in a suitable position to have their heads chopped off by the defendants as they emerged into the interior.

Then there is the loch. This is 10 miles long and is guarded to the south-east by Ben Hope which rears 3,000 ft above Beat 1 of the South End fishery. The northernmost end of the loch narrows into the Hope River. There are a few cottages and houses there, close to the water level and protecting forests, and the 700-ft Ben Arnaboll rises above the far shore to the west. One and a half miles to the north is the sea. Cape Wrath is 25 miles north-west as the herring gull flies.

At Hope I met Sam Boileau, whose family owns the Hope Estate. He is in charge of fishing arrangements. The loch, so far as fishing is concerned, is divided into three sections: North End, Middle Bay and South End. A total of eleven boats fish the loch. The estate has four boats on the North End. The Altnaharra Hotel rents two boats on the South End and four on Middle Bay. The eleventh is rented from the estate by the owner of the Strathmore Estate.

The booking of the four boats retained by the estate is under the control of Ian MacDonald, the estate gamekeeper, whose address and telephone

Dapping on South End.

number are given under 'Finding sea-trout Fishing' at the end of the book. They are let by the week, half week or day. Hope River lets are arranged by the Boileau family to whom enquirers will be referred by Ian. Anglers on the loch and the river can stay in local bed and breakfasts, but the main base is the Altnaharra Hotel, a renowned anglers' centre for the area.

Sam is encouraged by recent loch sea-trout catches, which went through lean seasons in the early 1990s, dropping to about 350 fish. A substantial recovery has taken place, first to approximately 500 in 1995, and then to not far short of 900 in 1996, excluding finnock, which are returned.

Anglers fishing the North End usually dap with 18-ft rods, floss lines and buzzy flies such as the Blue Zulu. It is rare for the loch to be windless, or for the wind to be too strong, but at the north end a strong southerly can make the water rough and lead to caution in putting out a boat.

Sam is taking over the long-term management of the fishing from Simon and Penny Murch. They have done a great deal to promote fishery improvement policies on Loch Hope and the welfare of the sea-trout, but they are now returning to England. When I arrived at Loch Hope, tired and hungry after a long drive, they entertained Sam and me to dinner and the substantial fruits of the sea – Loch Eriboll prawns.

Sam has been coming to the loch since the age of three, and caught his first sea-trout in the river when he was eight on a Low Water Hairy Mary. The rod was suited to his physique: 6 ft of carbon fibre. 'I hooked this fish and was so surprised that I screamed. My father, who was fishing just around the corner, came sprinting up the river to help. He was somewhat shirty to have been summoned for a finnock.'

The next fish, a 5½-lb grilse, came in late July after an interval of six years, and on the same rod. The river was again the scene, and the place the Gratel Run. Being netless, a small 14-year-old, and by himself, it was a terrifying experience. He

beached the fish, grabbed it by the tail, drew it away from the water, and sat on it.

His best sea-trout, of 4 lb, came at dusk to a single-hooked buzzy fly, the Zulu, fished as the tide started to flow. Saltwater backs up the river to about half of its 1¼ mile length. The system is to study the tide tables, then fish as the level is on the make, moving up the river to cast on each pool as the level starts to rise.

When I met Ian MacDonald, the estate gamekeeper, on 29 September 1996 it was a moment or two before we could hear ourselves speak, owing to the welcome of his dogs. These ran along the fence enclosing his large cottage and kennels from sheep grazing the lochside. The cottage's situation is superb – close to the water and just upstream of the bridge where the loch runs out into the 1¼-mile long Hope River. Surrounding heather- and pine-covered hills and mountains guard the house. The main canine welcome was from a large black labrador, five years of age at the time and strong enough to retrieve a shot mallard from the loch. There were three smaller members of the pack, and their task is foxing. Ian showed me the game larder, where a stag hung ready for collection by the dealer's van, and where two more would be gathered from the hill in the next two days.

Living in the wilds of Scotland, having migrated north 11 years ago from Grantown-on-Spey, Ian is a man of many sporting skills: stalking, woodcock and duck shooting and flighting, and assisting falconers at grouse. Then there is the fishing. As I have said, the Hope Estate's four boats are Ian's responsibility. Anglers are advised to bring their own anchors and drogues, and are requested to enter their catch in the record book in the fishing shed. At one time he issued catch record cards, but these were not always completed and returned. He does not arrange ghillies for the boats, but provides anglers with an informative map of the water.

The 1996 season was one of drought. Some rain had fallen recently and the loch had started

A dapping fly held on a cork behind the reel keeps the hook away from the floss blow line.

When fishing the river for sea-trout, Ian likes to be just above the tide: half an hour as it starts to flow, and the final half-hour of the ebb. His favourite fly is the Goat's Toe (John Veniard's dressing).

Body: Bronze peacock herl
Ribs: Scarlet floss silk
Tail: Scarlet wool
Hackle: Green peacock breast feather with fairly long fibres.
Hook: No 8 single

The Altnaharra Hotel is owned by Anne and Daniel Tüscher, who arrange fishing for guests on the rivers Mudale, Strathmore, Borgie, Halladale and Shin, and also many brown-trout lochs. The jewels in their crown are the six boats they rent from the Hope Estate on the loch, two on the South End and four on Middle Bay. The boats on South End do not need to be equipped with outboard motors, as the beats are within rowing distance of the landing bay. Outboards are provided for those fishing Middle Bay. It is recommended that anglers wear life-jackets and do not stand up in a boat.

Daniel confirmed the rise in sea-trout catches that had taken place in 1996. Their first fish came on 17 June, marking the middle of that month as the start of the loch season. The boats then took 201 sea-trout to the end of July, 101 in August in bright, hot, difficult conditions, and 200 in September. He offered me a boat and Jimmy Bain as ghillie on the final day of the season, 30 September. As we caught and returned four finnock and I kept and ate one sea-trout of 1½ lb, his September total was the same as July. The season thus produced over 500 sea-trout (not counting finnock which were returned), compared with 298 in 1995.

Finnock are always put back into the loch. It used to be the practice to return all sea-trout under 1¼ lb, but in the low seasons of the early 1990s this was raised to 1½ lb. The improved catches now experienced owe much to this

to rise, but was still low for the time of year. But as Sam said, the dry summer was not a hindrance to the loch fishing, in fact catches had improved substantially over the previous year. Sea-trout claw their way up the Hope river in the lowest water conditions, although a high tide helps them on their way. Large sea-trout start to enter in May. Finnock, of which Ian says there are three main runs, arrive in July, or even late June, but their entry is over by mid-September. Salmon come in when the river is in spate, but Ian has known of only two taken in ten years from the North End loch beats; salmon fishing is confined to the river.

Most of his anglers fish the dap. Occasionally, in a flat calm, a sea-trout will take a dry fly cast out and left to rest undisturbed upon the water, the North End being closest of the three Loch Hope sections to the tide, its sea-trout are fresh and free risers. There are a few brown trout, but these are not pursued with intent. The largest brown Ian has seen was a 5-lb ferox which took a wet fly about five years ago.

If you come to fish the North End of the loch pray for a southerly wind. This blows straight up the loch and makes for good dapping. Call upon the Lord not to send you a north-wester off Loch Eriboll, for circular gusts will whirl your dap in all directions.

restraint as the spawning cycle is between 3½–4½ years.

Jimmy took 84 sea-trout to his boat and returned well over 100 finnock. His rods also caught two salmon of 8 lb and 7 lb. A number of small brown trout are taken and, occasionally, a very large one, like that of the Revd Cant from Orkney – his prize was a 5½-lb brown caught in the third week of September. I inspected this magnificent fish in the rod-room deep freeze.

Jimmy likes his rods to dap. On my visit he provided me with an 18-ft carbon-fibre telescopic rod. The reel was a Shakespeare Beaulite filled with 20-lb monofilament to the end of which was knotted 10 ft of nylon floss. A short piece of blow line should not be attached to the end of a dressed salmon or trout fly line. Such lines are too heavy, do not blow out in the wind and tend to run back down the rod line guides, thus pulling in the floss, and the whole lot forms a bundle on the boat floorboards. The fly should be suspended on 4 ft of 8-lb nylon tied to the end of the floss.

The rods are not extended whilst rowing or motoring to the allocated beat, but the outfit is already assembled. This means that the floss and short leader are threaded through the line guides, the fly is tied on, and the hook pricked into a wine bottle cork taped to the rod butt behind the reel.

Pumping out the boat at the start of the day.

A plastic electric conduit placed over thole pins prevents the oars clattering and frightening fish by vibration.

This arrangement allows the rod to be extended vertically, section after section being pulled out, on arrival at the beat, the line being pulled off the reel simultaneously, whilst the angler remains seated. Floss line catches on any wood splinter, nail, boot stud, button or hook point, threads are pulled out and the whole is weakened. So the cork behind the reel mounting keeps the fly hook away from the floss line in front of the reel.

The fly should not be knotted to the leader by a tucked half blood, which can turn sideways to the eye of the hook. This would allow the fly to alight on the water with the hook parallel to the surface whilst the leader is vertical. Instead, use a Turle knot to ensure that the hook is beneath the suspended dapping fly and is thus the first part of the fly to encounter a rising fish.

There are many dapping flies: Loch Ordie, Blue Zulu, Fore & Aft, Black Pennell, and artificial or natural Daddy Long Legs. Jimmy prefers a dark fly on a bright day, but whatever the pattern you use, keep changing it if it does not bring success. Flies should be waterproofed by immersion in the liquid Mucilin bottle. As Jimmy says, 'Some anglers use a spray floatant, but they waste most of it in the air and this goes against the grain with me, being a mean Scot.'

I spent a few hours with Jimmy in his boat. The day was overcast and we fished the dap, returning a number of finnock. This augured well for the following year, as they would spawn and then return as full sea-trout after a second visit to the sea. The summit of Ben Hope was invisible, wreathed in mist and low cloud. Jimmy said: 'Herbert MacDonald, who died four years ago, and was a ghillie here for many seasons, said "When there is mist on the cap of the Ben you'll not catch many fish."' This was not my experience for, besides returning little fish and having large ones boil at the fly, I took a 1½-lb sea-trout

Finnock are returned.

back to the cottage where I was staying, and cooked it for supper.

Jimmy does not believe a rod needs to be particularly long for wet fly fishing. Rods of 10 or 11 ft have become fashionable, or even 12-ft drifters. Of course a long rod enables droppers to be dibbled across the water surface on the retrieve, and as the rod is lifted into the back cast. But more important, in his opinion, is delicacy. The line must be laid on the water without a splash, and this is accomplished just as well with a 9- or 10-ft rod. A floating line is normal, with an 8-lb monofilament leader, untapered, straight off the spool. An untapered length is possible, as casting is almost always down-wind. The leader ought to be long, 10 or 11 ft. Two droppers should be added to the point fly, formed by waterknots. Jimmy's first choice for the point is the Black Pennell, but rods can then follow their own ideas for droppers: Peter Ross, Mallard & Claret, Grouse & Red and others of that style. The hook size is generally No 10 or No 12, depending on the clarity of the water and the roughness of the surface.

Jimmy has a lot of time for women anglers. 'They are more persistent. They succeed. Some are very good indeed.' He described the co-operative system of a couple who fished from his boat. The lady dapped; the husband fished a team of wet flies. It is probably true that the dap brings up more fish from the depths than the wet fly. It is also a fact that many miss the dapped fly as it scuttles across the surface at speed, and some substantial fish boil beneath the dancing lure. When this happened to his wife's fly, the husband, quick as a flash, covered the area where the fish had moved with his wet-fly team. His reaction was so fast that at times he hooked the floss line, but more often it was sea-trout.

Jimmy told me of one experience he could not explain, and I could throw no light on the matter either. One summer, in the last week of July and the first week of August, he had in his boat an experienced and skilful angler who came to Altnaharra each year and shared a boat. One visit resulted in 32 good sea-trout to this man's rod. The next year he failed to catch a single fish, whilst his companion had reasonable success. As Jimmy said, 'I turned the boat around so that their ends were changed in relation to the drift – it made no difference. Those fish totally ignored his fly throughout that fortnight.'

One day he was surprised to find his boat surrounded by seagulls flapping about on the surface of the loch. 'They couldn't take off. It was the funniest thing I have seen in all my years. My rod was feeding them bread pellets soaked in Scotch. After a while their heads cleared and they took off, with a hangover I suppose.'

Glossary of Angling Terms

Adipose fin – small fin on the back of a game fish between the dorsal fin and the tail

AFTM Scale – defines the weight of a fly line

Alevin – fishlet with yolk sac which hatches from an ovum

Arlesley bomb – a weight incorporating a swivel

Backing – an additional length of strong thin line joined to, and beneath, the fly line on a reel

Backing up – a method of fishing the fly whilst moving from the tail to the head of a pool in a river

Bail arm – that part of a fixed-spool reel which gathers and winds the line onto the spool

Bank (in boat fishing) – an area of shallow water in a loch

Bank (of a river) – looking downstream, the right bank is to your right, the left bank to your left

Bass – a bag made of woven raffia for holding, transporting and keeping fish cool when wet

Blow line (also known as a floss line) – undressed fluffy line blown out by the wind from the tip of a long rod, to carry the fly over and dance upon the water when dapping from a boat

Bob fly – the fly closest to the butt of the leader, and thus the fly line, when a team of flies is being fished

Braided leader – 4-ft length of tapered braided nylon joined to the fly line, to which a length of monofilament, the tippet, is knotted; densities vary

Braided loop – braided nylon sleeve into which the end of the fly line is inserted; has a loop on the end for attachment of the leader

Burn – a small Scottish stream

Butt (of leader) – thickest part of a tapered leader where it joins the fly line

Butt (of rod) – the handle end

Chironomid – a midge

Crane fly – a daddy-long-legs

Collar – a short length of thick monofilament attached to the end of a fly line, to which the leader is joined

Creel – a wicker basket carried by angler to hold fish

Dropper – a second or third fly fished on a leader between the point and bob flies

Finnock – a small Scottish sea-trout on its first return to the river or loch from the sea

Fish – in Scotland, this refers to a salmon rather than a sea-trout or trout (an indefinite term)

Flight (hook mount) – a treble hook, wire (sometimes nylon) and swivel passing through the hollow centre of an artificial minnow

Floss line – see Blow line

Fry – a small young fish after the alevin stage

Gaff – a pointed hook on a shaft for landing large fish. Not always legal.

Gape – defines the gap measurement between the point and shank of a hook

Ghillie (gillie) – person who should have detailed knowledge of a river or loch and is employed to assist anglers

Grilse – a 'one-sea-winter' salmon

Groyne – a man-made protrusion from a river bank to create a fish lie

Gye net – a large salmon or sea-trout net carried on the back on a peal sling

Herling – a small sea-trout on its first return to the river from the sea

Kelt – a spawned salmon or sea-trout

Kype – the upward hook on the lower jaw of a cock fish

Leader (historically called a cast) – the length of nylon (used to be gut) joining the fly line to the tail (point) fly

Lie – a favoured place where fish rest in a river

Lure – a wide term embracing spinning baits, artificial flies, plugs etc

Mend – to move the fly line on the water, after the initial cast, by switching upstream (usual) or downstream (unusual) to decrease or increase the speed of passage of a fly across the river to the angler's bank

Mepp – a revolving spoon bait

Neck (of a river pool) – the narrow entrance where the river runs into the pool

Nymph (natural and artificial) – underwater stage in the life cycle of some orders of insects

Otter – a device to release spinning baits from the riverbed

Ova – the eggs of a fish

Parr – a small salmon or sea-trout, a few inches in length, in the initial stage of its life cycle, before smoltifying and going to sea

Paternoster – a method of fishing a spinning bait or worm slowly and close to the riverbed

Peal – West Country term for a sea-trout

Peal sling – a quick-release harness by which a Gye net is carried on the angler's back

Plug – an artificial vaned bait, usually fish-shaped, sometimes jointed, which moves about in a wriggling manner when retrieved by a spinning reel

Point fly – the fly at the end of a leader

Priest – a short truncheon with which to kill fish by hitting them on the head

Pupa – an immature stage of some flies

Rapala – a type of plug bait

Redd – a depression cut in gravel by fish in a riverbed in which a female deposits ova and where ova are fertilized by the milt of cock fish

Run-off – the downstream, tail end of a river pool

Shoalie, Schoolie – a small sea-trout on its first return to the river from the sea

School peal – see shoalie

Scissors – the point of the angle between the upper and lower jaws of a fish

Sea-lice – suckered lice found on the flanks and back of salmon and sea-trout when they enter the river from the sea; they drop off in fresh water after a few days.

Sea-trout – a migratory brown trout

Sewin – a Welsh term for a sea-trout

Shoot – when false casting with a fly line and making the final throw, passing extra line out through the line guides to obtain additional distance

Shooting head – the first 10 yd of a tapered fly line that is cut off and needle-knotted to special monofilament backing; enables long casts to be shot.

Skate (skid) – a fly crossing the river, or drawn over the surface of a loch, on top of, or in, the water surface film.

Sliced hook – type of hook with a barbed shank used in worm fishing to stop the worm sliding down the hook shank

Smolt – an immature salmon or sea-trout, silver in colour, migrating downriver in spring to enter the sea

Spate – the rise and fall of the water level in a river following rain in the catchment area

Spinner – a general term for a revolving artifical bait

Spinner (natural fly) – the second aerial and egg-laying stage of flies of the order *Ephemeroptera*.

Split cane – a rod of hexagon cross-section formed of six faced strips of cane bonded or silk-wrapped together

Spoon – a type of spinning bait

Spring tide – high tide occurring at full and new moons

Stale fish – a salmon or sea-trout which has been in fresh water for some months after entry from the sea; the term is most frequently used in autumn and is likely to refer to a dark or red fish, many of which should be returned to the water

Stickle – a shallow section of a river between two pools

Tail (of a pool) – the downstream end

Tail fly – see Point fly

Tailer – wire noose to land salmon

Throat (of a river pool) – see Neck

Tippet – the point section of monofilament of a leader

Toby – a type of spoon bait

Trace – a short length, usually about 1 m, of nylon between the swivel at the end of a spinning line and the bait

UDN – ulcerative dermal necrosis, a fish skin disease

Wake lure – a floating fly for sea-trout which skids across the water surface of a river creating a 'V' wake

Walk up – a method of persuading a hooked fish, usually a salmon, to move upstream

Weight-forward fly line – a line tapered only at the front end where the weight is concentrated; the greater length of the line is of small diameter to facilitate shooting and thus distance casting

Wind knot – a knot formed unintentionally in the leader whilst casting; weakens the leader

Wye weight – a weight used in salmon and sea-trout natural or artificial bait fishing; it has a metal loop at one end for line attachment and a swivel at the other to which the trace is knotted

Finding Sea-trout Fishing

The River Taw

High Bullen Hotel
Chittlehamholt
North Devon
Tel: 01769 540561

Fox & Hounds Hotel
Eggesford
Chulmleigh
Mid-Devon
Tel: 01769 580345

Peter Huntington
Hobbs Wood Cottage
Charles
Brayford
Barnstaple
North Devon
01598 760430

The River Teign

Roddy Rae
Half Stone Sporting Agency
6 Hescane Park
Cheriton Bishop
Devon
Tel: 01647 24643

Upper Teign Fishing Association
Permits from:

Angler's Rest Inn
Fingle Bridge
Drewsteignton
Devon
or
Bowden's Shop
The Square
Chagford
Devon

Lower Teign Fishing Association
Permits from:
Drum Sports
47 Courtenay Street
Newton Abbot
South Devon
01626 65333

The River Dovey

The Brigands Inn Hotel
Mallwyd
Machynlleth
Powys
Tel: 01650 531208

New Dovey Fishery Association
Tickets from:
T.A. Hughes, Newsagent
Penralit Street
Machynlleth
Powys

or
The Post Office
Cemmaes
between Mallwyd and Machynlleth
or
Cemmaes Garage

The River Towy

Abercothi and Golden Grove Fisheries
Hamdden Ltd
Plas-y-Ffynnon
Ffordd Cambria
Aberbonddu
Powys
Tel: 01874 623181

Also many associations in the area listed in *The Trout & Salmon Guide to Fishing in Wales* (Ed. Pat O'Reilly)

The River Fowey

Lanhydrock Angling Association
Lanhydrock Estate Office
Lanhydrock
Bodmin
Cornwall.
Tel: 01208 74281

Liskeard & District Angling Club
Many ticket sales outlets listed in the West Country Tourist Board *Guide to Angling in the South West* obtainable by telephoning the board at Exeter on 01392 442008

The Hampshire Avon

The Royalty Fishery
Head Bailiff:
Alan Godfrey
2 Avon Buildings
Christchurch
Dorset
Tel: 01202 485262

Bookings for the Bridge Pool are by written application in February to the Fishery Manager, address as above.
Tickets are also available from:
Davis Fishing Tackle Shop
75 Bargates
Christchurch
Dorset
Tel: 01202 485169

The Rivers Tamar and Lyd

Arundel Arms Hotel
Lifton
Devon
Tel: 01566 784263

Launceston Anglers' Association
Permits from:
Homeleigh Garden Centre
Dutson
Launceston
Cornwall.

Endsleigh House Hotel
Milton Abbot
Tavistock
Devon
Tel: 01822 87248
Permits only to residents

The Border Esk

Anthony King
Nethernock
Bentpath
Nr Langholm
Dumfries and Galloway
Tel: 01387 370288

The Esk and Liddle Fisheries
Head River Watcher:
George Graham
The Old School

151

Hagg-on-Esk
Canonbie
Dumfries and Galloway
Tel: 01387 371416
Also Stevenson & Johnstone WS
Bank of Scotland Buildings
Langholm
Dumfries and Galloway
They issue a guide to callers.
Tel: 01387 380248

Tanlawhill Estate
John Jewitt
Lyneholm House
Nr Langholm
Dumfries and Galloway
Tel: 01387 370 228

The River Spey

The Strathspey Angling Improvement Association
Tickets available only from:
Mortimers
3 High Street
Grantown-on-Spey
Moray
Tel: 01479 872684

REFFIS guide service:
David Herbert
Parkburn Guest House
Grantown-on-Spey
Moray
Tel: 01479 873116

Kincardine Water:
Revack Estate Office
Nethybridge
Inverness-shire
Tel: 01479 821377

A guide to available Spey Valley fishing is issued by:
Grantown-on-Spey Tourist Information Centre
54 High Street
Grantown-on-Spey
Moray
Tel: 01479 872773

The following are useful Spey fishery contact telephone numbers:
Strathspey Estate Office 01479 872529
Abernethy Angling Improvement Association 01479 98372
Castle Grant Estate Office 01479 872529
Tulchan Sporting Estate Ltd 01807 510200
Ballendalloch Estate 01807 500205
Carron & Laggan, c/o Bidwells 01463 715585
Easter Elchies, Upper Arndilly, c/o Bidwells 01463 715585
Lower Wester Elchies, c/o Finlayson Hughes 01738 630926
Delfur, Rothes & Aikenway 01340 871488
Delagyle Beat, c/o Savills 01356 221187
Gordon Castle & Speymouth 01343 820244
Fochabers Angling Association 01343 820327
Speymouth Angling Association 01343 820636

Loch Hope

For North End
Ian Macdonald
The Keepers Cottage
The Hope Estate
Hope
Sutherland
Tel: 01847 601272

For South End and Middle Bay:
Altnaharra Hotel
By Lairg
Sutherland
Tel: 01549 411222

Sea-trout Fishing Instruction

The Register of Experienced Fly Fishing Instructors & Schools (REFFIS) has instructors, schools and guides throughout Britain and Ireland. For information on members offering sea-trout fishing instruction and lets, telephone:

Chairman: Charles Bingham 01822 613899
Vice-Chairman: Roddy Rae 01647 24643
Secretary: Richard Slocock 01305 848460
For a *REFFIS Directory of Instructors and Guides* telephone Tony King on 01387 370288.

Useful Knots

Reel to backing

Arbor knot

This knot is suitable for both monofilament and braided backing.

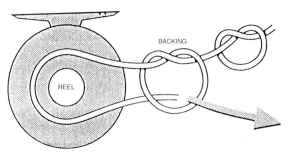

Backing to fly line

Albright knot

Used to join braided backing to the fly line. This is the bulkiest of the three alternative knots in this position, and is one reason why monofilament backing is preferable.

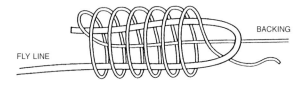

Needle knot

This can only be used for monofilament thin enough to pass into the core of the fly line. Use 20lb monofilament, cutting the end on a slant to ease introduction into the fly line. The diameter of needles needs to be chosen with care, but the needles do not need to be heated to establish a suitable hole. This is the best and smoothest knot, passing without disturbance through the rod line guides. In sea-trout fishing it is also my choice for joining the fly line to the butt of the leader.

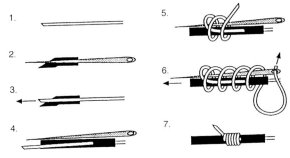

Nail knot

For use when the monofilament backing is too thick to pass into the core of a thin fly line. A fat needle is required. The result is not as smooth as the needle knot.

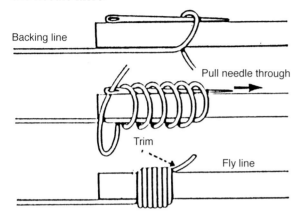

Fly line to leader

Needle knot

Already described. Pass 1 ft of 20lb monofilament into the core of the fly line; join this with a blood knot to the butt of the leader. This is the most desirable line/leader junction for sea-trout fishing in the dark.

Loop-to-loop

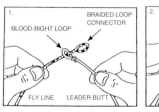
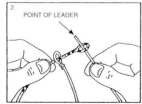
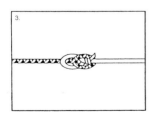

For joining a braided loop on the end of the fly line to the blood-bight loop on the butt of a knot-less tapered leader, or home-made sectional leader. An inferior choice in sea-trout fishing to the needle knot, but good for daylight fishing when one is able to see that the junction is kept outside the top of the rod. Good for trout fishing and the rapid changing of leaders.

Leader construction and droppers

Blood-bight loop

To form a loop on the butt end of a homemade leader in order to join 'loop-to-loop' with a braided loop on the end of a fly line.

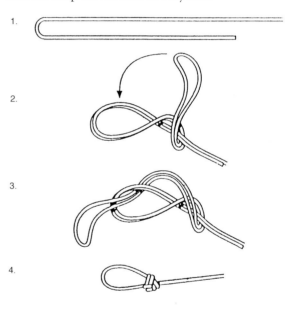

Water knot
For making tapered leaders and joining lengths of nylon where one length is short. One end, the upper, may be left about 4 inches long, and pointing upwards towards the rod tip, to form a dropper.

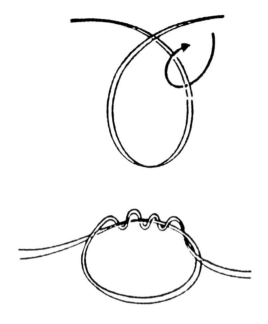

Blood knot
Used to join sections of nylon when making leaders. Lengths to be joined should not be of widely disimilar diameters or the knot will not tighten. To add a dropper, leave one end of the knot extending a few inches after construction,

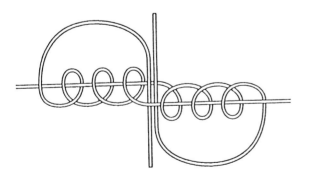

whilst trimming the other end close to the knot. The end to be left as a dropper should be the continuation of the section above the knot; in the unlikely event of the knot coming undone whilst playing a fish, the quarry would still be attached. The knot should be moistened in the mouth before tightening.

Leader to fly–eyed

Two-Turn Turle
The best knot for eyed flies. The loop, passing around the shank of the hook immediately behind the eye of the fly, keeps the fly in line with the leader. When tying eyed flies a small neck should be left behind the eye to accommodate this loop. Too many dressers wind their tying silk thickly right up to the back of the eye of the fly – this prevents use of the Turle.

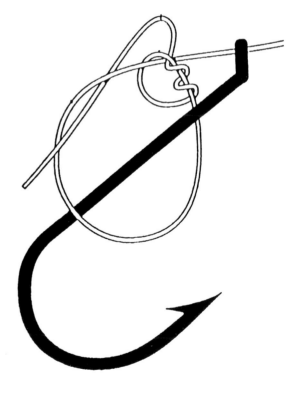

Leader to fly – tube fly and spinning baits

Tucked half-blood

This should not be favoured for eyed flies as the knot can slide around the perimeter of the metal eye of the fly. This may cause the fly to fish at an angle to the leader. It must be used to attach the 'in line with the shank' eyes of treble hooks used in tube flies, or where the dresser of the fly has not left a neck to an eyed fly to take the loop of the Turle.

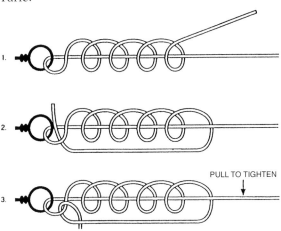

Wind knot

A wind knot is a single turn formed unintentionally in a leader whilst casting. It reduces the breaking strength of nylon by about 50%. The faulty section of the leader should be replaced or, at the least, the knot snapped with a jerk and the ends joined with a blood knot.

Index